WING C

M A R T I A L   A R T S

WING CHUN
MARTIAL ARTS

PRINCIPLES & TECHNIQUES

YIP CHUN
with
Danny Connor

SAMUEL WEISER, INC.

York Beach, Maine

First published in the United States in 1993 by
Samuel Weiser, Inc.
Box 612
York Beach, Maine 03910

99 98
10 9 8 7 6 5 4 3

Library of Congress Cataloging-in-Publication Data

Yip, Chun.
    Wing chun martial arts : principles and techniques--skill and phi-
losophy / by Yip Chun with Danny Connor.
          p.   cm.
    Rev. ed. of: Wing chun. 1992.
    1. Kung fu.   I. Connor, Danny.   II. Yip, Chun.   Wing chun.
III. Title.
GV1114.7.Y37   1993
796.8'159--dc20   93-9998
                                                                CIP

ISBN 0-87728-796-1
MG

Cover photographs by Alan Seabright. Used by kind permission.

Typeset in 10/13 Palatino

Printed in the United States of America

The paper used in this publication meets the minimum requirements of
the American National Standard for Permanence of Paper for Printed
Library Materials Z39.48-1984.

CONTENTS

ACKNOWLEDGEMENTS

The authors would like to thank Mr Samuel Kwok, chief instructor of the Wing Chun Athletic Association, for his cooperation in the production of this book.

Also his senior student Shaun Rawcliffe for assisting with the photographs and for his help in the development of the text.

Warren Szeto, Thomas Chan and Patrick Leung for interpretation (Hong Kong).

Samuel Kwok, Ken Lau, Wan Wo Kwok and Mo Yeu Fong for translation (UK).

Archie Brahms for the translation of Confucius.

Fung Kam Hing, Guandong China for the calligraphy.

PREFACE

I am honoured to have been requested by Grandmaster Yip Chun to help in the putting together of this book. To my mind, Yip Chun is a man of many talents. He is, in the classical Chinese mould, a 'man of excellencies'. Apart from his documented martial skills, he is a poet, painter, calligrapher, musician and philosopher. He has worked as a journalist, accountant, museum curator, teacher and for ten years of his life was caught up in the Cultural Revolution performing back-breaking work. He is an avid walker and has impishly invited a number of Kung Fu masters to a mountain walk and then to practise 'sticking hands' at the end of it. No one as yet has taken up this challenge.

His technique is also formidable at sea level. He lives in Hong Kong where he teaches. He also travels throughout the world giving seminars/lectures to those who have acquired a taste for quality.

Yip Chun stands at only 5ft 2ins, and weighs 120lbs; he is now sixty-eight years old, yet the skills inherited from his father Yip Man still flow, undiminished by the passing of time.

Danny Connor 1992

Rooftop training in Hong Kong

INTRODUCTION

Legend has it that Wing Chun means 'beautiful springtime' and is said to be the name of a woman who reputedly studied a martial art from a Buddhist nun named Ng Mui. Legend has it that Madam Wing Chun learned it to repel a suitor who wished to take her for his wife and possess her inheritance. She studied for 100 days and when he came to claim her she repelled him with her martial skill. She later married someone of her own choosing, who learned from her skills and sold them to other martial arts instructors.

While the above cannot be proven, it can be said that the techniques are eminently suited to females and those of small stature.

Wing Chun falls into the category known as Southern Shaolin Boxing (fast hands, strong legs), yet it employs 'softness' within its dynamic, which is characterised by a method of practice known as Chi Sau (a method of sticking or clinging arms practice with a partner to develop the techniques that appear in the forms).

But Wing Chun practice is more than just a better form of self-defence. It has a 'Chineseness' which makes it fascinating. The character 'Chung' means central, and the characters for China (central kingdom) embrace this understanding. Whilst the Western world studied sciences that dealt with the largest and smallest of things, the Chinese ventured into the area of harmony and balance (in Buddhist theory, 'the middle way').

Many people regard Wing Chun as a Buddhist art, with techniques such as fut sau or budda hand within the practice. But this is not necessarily proof since for millenia the Chinese have comfortably lived with the concepts of Taoism, Confucianism and Buddhism – a trinity of thought that underpins 'Chineseness'. Tai Chi, for example, claims Taoist theory (or yin-yang) as the spiritual principle or dialectic, yet even Tai Chi techniques have names such as 'Buddha's attendant pounds the mortar', attesting to the cross-fertilisation within Chinese culture.

Frankly all martial arts employ the yin-yang theory in different ways.

The Shaolin Temple in Hunan Province was Buddhist and is probably the most famous icon for Chinese martial arts. Yet it lies close to Chen village – the home of Tai Chi.

Yip Chun first drew my attention to a small volume of Confucius called *Chung Yung* or *The Doctrine of the Mean* in Hong Kong a few years ago. It was whilst reading about 'the shaping of an axe handle' that Wing Chun Chi Sau practice became for me an embodiment of what Confucius was saying 2500 years ago. The book deals with human relationships, and the quote 'do not do unto others that which you would not have them do unto you' has been mirrored in later philosophies and is also advice for all those who learn how to play Chi Sau.

Anyone could have made the connection, but it took Yip Chun with his consummate skill and awareness to offer to the ever widening clan of Wing Chun a moral guide, a tome that may be studied. It is a tireless piece, with each page offering a mirror and guide to one's own development. It addresses all who read it.

This book seeks to explore the centre line principle of Wing Chun complemented by Confucian theory as expounded in *The Doctrine of the Mean*. It is a moral guide for instructors and students alike. For the first time, it is presented for those wishing to understand the philosophy and practice of Wing Chun.

'Brief is beautiful' is the motto of Wing Chun, a martial art which follows a centre line theory and regards the body as a matrix of gates.

The movements practised in the forms, which I prefer to regard as honing or exercise methods, were refined by Yip Man, who brought Wing Chun to Hong Kong from Fatshan city in China.

Yip Chun, the eldest son of Yip Man, was told by his father that if Wing Chun forms could be simplified without losing skill they would be developing the art to a higher level. No one has managed to do so to date. It seems that many have added to the style but few have been able to simplify it.

This aim towards a simpler, functionalist approach has a particular intellectual appeal to some people. It is at the very centre of the sticking hands system, which allows the techniques learned to be fed into the practice, safely eliminating dangerous techniques such as finger thrusting, elbow strikes and striking the face of a partner. The aim of Chi Sau is to conserve energy and control your opponent's movements through correct application of technique and sensitivity to another's intentions.

Yip Chun with Samuel Kwok at one of the many seminars held in the UK

AN INTERVIEW WITH

YIP CHUN

In 1989 I was lucky enough to be able to interview Yip Chun in China for a magazine article. The following is an adaptation of that article.

The smell of petrol was everywhere. There I was sitting in a taxi, waiting at a filling station in Canton, China. I was accompanying Yip Chun to Fatshan province to visit the birthplace of his father, Yip Man. I was researching the background of Wing Chun with Yip Chun, whom I had come to Hong Kong to study with and ask many questions. Master Yip Chun is 5ft 2ins, 120lbs, a slight man of sixty-eight years. A scholar and accountant by training, he is also the inheritor of the skills of his late, great father, Yip Man. A year earlier I had made a video training film of Yip Chun and since that time I had felt he was a master in the truest sense of the word. I have seen him perform his skills of sticking hands both in England and Hong Kong, where none could dent his ability. He conducts himself as a gentleman and refrained from making criticism of other teachers and masters throughout the world. I was training and conducting an extended interview for one month in Hong Kong and China, and that is how I happened to be sitting in the back seat of the taxi with an interpreter, and the master was sitting in the front directing the way. Now I saw the master put his pipe to his mouth and with his other hand bring the lighter to it. The smell of the gasoline was overpowering and I began to worry that I might

end up as a telegram home, so I shouted, 'No, don't light it.' He looked up a little surprised at this noisy foreigner. Our interpreter meanwhile had left the vehicle to stretch his legs, which severely limited the conversation. The master blinked and wound the window down as if to release the smoke from his now almost lit pipe. I began sniffing and waving my hand under my nose to explain the smell. He nodded in what I took to be agreement, yet continued to attempt to light his pipe after tapping down the tobacco.

Determined not to end my days in this kamikaze taxi time bomb, I made a lunge for his hand holding the lighter. Just as my hand reached his wrist, he disengaged it with a flick of the wrist and a wry smile, with a look that seemed to be figuring I was giving him a test. I made another attempt and failed to secure any grip. I was beginning to become aware of the depth of my predicament – here I was trying to keep us alive by arm wrestling a great Kung Fu master. I remembered the many times in Chi Sau practice that he could join me with one hand in bong sau position and pepper my chest with little flicks of his other fist to indicate what he could be doing. He now seemed to see it as a game of grab his wrist and light his pipe at the same time. I began blowing in desperation at the lighter to indicate I wouldn't let him light it. Just then the interpreter re-entered the car.

'What are you trying to do to the master?' he said,

suspiciously.

'I'm trying to avoid us getting to Fatshan by air,' I replied.

After a translation we all had a good laugh and sped down the road, past the green rice paddies and dusty roads and grey buildings that gave a romantic backdrop to my questions and the master's replies. I had already cleared the ground in advance with the master and apologised that my questions might seem brash and irrelevant, but he waved this aside and told me to fire away.

What makes a person skilled in Kung Fu?

I know Wing Chun and speak from my experience of studying, teaching and observing it. A student must learn to use force correctly. In some styles of Kung Fu and Karate there is a tendency to use force all the time and this limits the development of control. Knowing the right moment to use force is of great importance and must be learned if one is to succeed. The use of and release of force. The non-understanding of this point is the lack of progress that many people experience, a simple point, but one which is the key to success.

Could you give me some information on the history of Wing Chun?

Wing Chun history is well-documented, some fact, some fiction. In the Sung dynasty there lived a man who was an expert and also schooled in Confucian thoughts. Wong Yung Min was his name and he was much drawn to the theory that to achieve something there are two things involved: theory and practice. Theory is the knowledge and practice means action.

This does not mean just mixing the two points together. What is meant is that during the practice, further theories may emerge and thus, like the yin-yang principle, it becomes knowledge, action, knowledge, action continuously developing. Without practice knowledge is useless, and after practice you must seek more knowledge to develop the art.

Do you feel that students of Wing Chun can benefit from further study of Confucius?

Yes, indeed. I feel both students and teachers would do well to study Confucius; teachers for the examples of leadership, and students to develop a philosophy that is embraced with Chi Sau practice. I feel that for some time the image of Wing Chun has been as a street-fighting art and instructors have failed to instil any moral philosophy into their practice. Tai Chi lays claim to Taoist theory, Shaolin claims its roots in Buddhist temples.

I urge all students of Wing Chun to study Chung Yung and through it understand the true theory and philosophy of Wing Chun. This is the missing piece for many students and will enrich their lives. Through the practice of Chi Sau (action) and Chung Yung (theory), they will continue to develop.

The taxi sped onward as Yip Chun expounded on these theories and principles. Slowly the traffic ahead brought us to a standstill by the side of the road. A small river ran parallel with occasional small concrete slabs that acted as bridges into the rice fields which stretched on to mountains in the distance.

We got out to stretch our legs and attempt to see what was causing the hold-up. Happening to find myself on one of these concrete slabs with the master, I was surprised to hear him say, 'Chi Sau?' 'Sure,' I said, and we began a little practice.

Playing sticking hands with the master is always a learning process, but doing it on a bridge added a piquancy I had not previously experienced. As soon as we began I realised that at any time I could be taking a dive into a suspicious-looking river six feet below. Although it was not truly dangerous I felt I could end up very wet and uncomfortable. We also had accumulated a number of Chinese spectators who found the spectacle fascinating. Although I speak no Cantonese, by the shouts I heard I figured they were calling on him to knock me into the water.

There were whoops of joy as my footing

neared the edge of the bridge, but as the traffic began moving all interest in my fate disappeared and we returned to the car to continue the journey.

Danny Connor

The authors, Danny Connor and Yip Chun

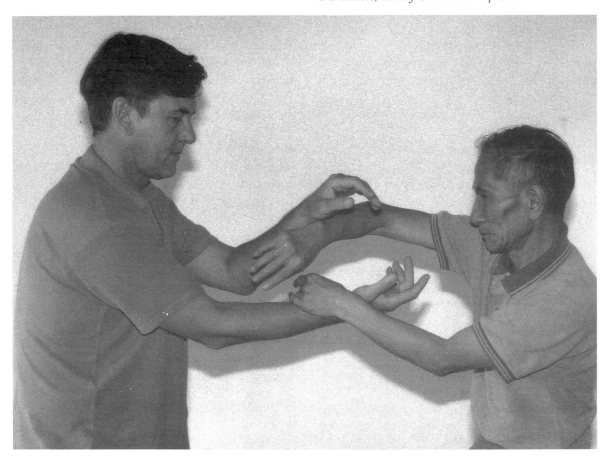

STUDYING WITH
YIP CHUN

I must say that I found the camaraderie amongst Yip Chun's students quite unique and I'm sure that this attitude comes from Yip Chun himself. As he told me many times, 'There are no secrets in Wing Chun.' It's all down to whether you're technically ready to make the next step, whether you can absorb the technique; and sometimes that technique may be just a fraction of a movement, hardly perceptible but it may neutralise a whole range of blows hailing down on you, such is the precision of the technique employed in Wing Chun.

Yip Chun teaches at Sha Tin Town Hall (HK), his home, or at his students' homes; he prefers to teach privately, where he can supervise and coach the students.

You don't see many of the students practising the forms during class at his home since Yip Man believed that they can practice those in their own time. When the students come to visit the master they come to learn and develop their skills and this is done through Chi Sau practice and plenty of it. There are reports of 1½ hours of almost continuous practice, and this refines a skill until it finds its way into the bone.

Master Yip's apartment is located on the 21st floor in one of those huge apartment blocks for which Hong Kong is famous. His students make the trek regularly, week in and week out; the relationship between master and students is casual, lacking the formality of many martial arts, but when it gets down to the nitty gritty, he is revered and well loved by all his students, many of whom have had disappointing experiences previously. It is to his credit that his students never leave to find more advanced instruction, for I feel there is none to match his. The skill he has transmitted to them is formidable and yet in the backdrop of simple domestic surroundings, the highest levels of the art are practised, discussed, analysed and remembered. Surely this is how the martial arts were originally taught! In an atmosphere in which the practice enriches, strengthens and develops the individual and in turn raises the cultural level of the society.

In the same way as an individual may study and practise music, when you are in the presence of a master you perform the techniques not the scales, which are for solo practice and left to your own time. When you are with the master the purpose is to develop and hone your skill in an alive situation, and when you stick hands with some of Yip Chun's senior students you know that at any given time they can disassemble your defence whenever they wish. In a way the geometry reaches higher and higher levels, but without the step-by-step progression of techniques and the sound training of those principles, there is the likelihood of leaving an opening in your technique which invites anyone to rush in like customers in a bargain sale.

What makes Wing Chun so unique? I would say that the main thing is in the approach, which surely comes from the master. At Master Yip Chun's house he takes in students in small groups to supervise their Chi Sau training, and when the students reach a point where they cannot contend with certain techniques he steps in and explains the problem, and gives five ways in which to avoid it and another five ways to get out of it. Really it all depends on your ability to absorb and understand the value of what you're being shown.

One evening I was invited by Master Yip and one of his senior students, Thomas, whom the master had described as very good, to have some Chi Sau techniques explained to me.

'Two hands but only one brain,' the master explained through Thomas. 'If I can draw your attention to one side then the other side is empty and I can then enter your defence,' Thomas said, illustrating this by splintering my attempts to defend. Able to blister through most of my attempts he generously said that he wouldn't punch me in the face. I began to wonder what he had in store for me; basically it was to show

Yip Chun and Danny Connor practising Chi Sau in the Ching Wu training hall, Fatshan, China, 1989

me that my defence technique had more leaks than a colander.

The master would sit giggling in his chair and occasionally get up to show me how to perhaps avoid some of the attacks, and then he would engage in Chi Sau with Thomas to illustrate how I might defend, and whereas I could do nothing, he was able to control and neutralise, with a laugh and a twinkle in his eye, which belied the quality of skill he was demonstrating.

Over the years I have been fortunate enough to acquire some of the skills of sticking hands. But when an almost seventy-year-old man weighing 120lbs takes off his glasses, puts down his pipe and decides to show you how, I'm really impressed. It was always a dream of mine that Kung Fu skill could be practised even by the old, and to have that demonstrated by one Yip Chun, son of Yip Man, for me have been moments of great pleasure.

Sticking hands with the master is a unique experience. Suddenly you find you can't move and his little fist is peppering your chest to let you know your defence has a marshmallow quality about it. And just as a jeweller who has a 'touch-stone' to define the gold content of an object, practising sticking hands with him will show you where the quality of your skill lies.

He is at each and every corner, ever ready for any eventuality; on a rapid change, he was there before you, he'd already been there thousands of times. It was like playing three dimensional chess: leave a little gap and he was through with

his palm tapping against the side of your face.

It's always embarrassing when you're made to feel inept, but Yip Chun does it with a smile and a laugh. There is no formality with him at all; after practising with you and leaving you in a heap of sweat and frustration, he picks up his pipe and sits there chomping away, not in the least out of breath. I must say it is both discouraging and illuminating. But something inside you says, 'If he can do it, why can't I?' and you begin to look with an awareness that you never felt before. Only at the moments when we are divested of ego do we truly learn, do we experience the distillation of skill, not only in the skin and muscle, but in the bone also. This is where Kung Fu is said to reside – not in competition and trophies that will dust and tarnish, but in the refinement of the skills, the art, call it what you will. The bottom line is that it has to prolong life and improve the quality of life.

So if you are invited to witness martial skills at any level, do so. Perhaps it may affect you deeply, who knows?

Danny Connor

Yip Chun has recently been invited to teach Wing Chun at Fatshan University, Guanzhou, China. The skill he has nurtured and preserved in Hong Kong will now be transplanted back to its place of origin. To date he is the only Kung Fu master to have been recognized in this way.

RESEARCHING THE
ORIGINS OF WING CHUN

Researching the history of Chinese Kung Fu is very difficult. This is due to a general lack of written records. For every Kung Fu clan, clan history was passed down orally from teacher to disciple. In due course, the disciple himself became a teacher, and taught his own disciples according to what his teacher passed down to him. History was thus passed down from generation to generation by word of mouth. This process involved some who were poorly educated, or had poor memories. There were also those who were not very interested in history, and were half-hearted in passing it down. Much was lost here. Some people borrowed from heroic characters in popular Chinese novels. They invented and exaggerated, and gave an air of myth and mystery to their founding fathers.

After several generations, the facts of history will be lost to hearsay and legend. Look at Southern Kung Fu clans. They padded their founders with fable, so all the founders either came from Siu Lam or Mo Dong. They were all Buddhist monks or nuns, or Taoist priests. So, suddenly, the glamour and hype of martial arts history was forced upon these peaceful places and fine people. It became a joke.

There are legends about the origins of the Wing Chun Kung Fu clan, retracing the period from Grandmaster Leung Jan. These are legends because there are no comprehensive written records. The general story goes like this:

Wing Chun was founded by Yim Wing Chun. Yim Wing Chun studied under Ng Mui of Siu Lam. This means that Wing Chun originated in Siu Lam. Yim Wing Chun married Leung Bok Chau, and she followed him back to his home town in Siu Hing, Canton. Wing Chun Kung Fu was passed down to Leung Jan through Leung Bok Chau. There are two different stories here. One says that Leung Bok Chau taught the techniques to Leung Lan Kwai, Wong Wah Bo, Leung Yee Tei and others. Wong Wah Bo and Leung Yee Tei then passed them on to Leung Jan. The other story says that Leung Jan and the others studied together under Leung Bok Chau. These stories about the origin of Wing Chun are consistent with an article by the late Grandmaster Yip Man on the origin of Wing Chun and also with a 1972 article I wrote for the 'Hong Kong Contemporary Martial Arts Circle'. They are also broadly in line with the general story on the origin of Wing Chun.

In 1982, I was in Fatshan, and paid a visit to Pang Nam (Blackface Nam). Pang Nam can be said to be a very senior member in the Fatshan Wing Chun Kung Fu clan. He was senior in years, rather than in the hierarchy. He was already eighty. Our discussion turned to the origin of Wing Chun, and Pang said, 'Wing Chun was brought to Fatshan from the North by a person called Tan-Sau Ng (Palm-up Arm Ng – a nickname). Yim Wing Chun is only a storybook character.' He sounded very sure.

Later, I unexpectedly unearthed some information about Tan-Sau Ng, recorded in old literature on the history of Chinese opera. This in-

formation is closely connected to the origin of Wing Chun.

There was a book by one Mak Siu Har – *A Study on the History of Cantonese Operas* (now kept in the Hong Kong City Hall Library). In it there was one paragraph, roughly as follows:

Before the reign of Yung Cheng (Manchu emperor, 1723–1736), the development of Cantonese opera was very limited. This was due to defective organisation

Jum dao

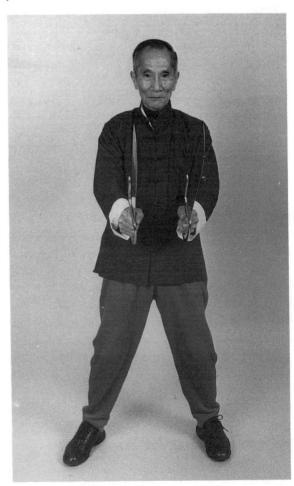

Baat Cham Dao – Eight cutting broadsword techniques. This form consists of 108 movements in eight sections, each section dealing with defence and counter against long, short or medium range weapons.

The knife form training complements the empty hand training as well as the wooden dummy techniques. It coordinates the movements of the stance, footwork, waist and upper body. Frequent practice develops energy in the elbow and wrist. The footwork and stances of Baat Cham Dao train the stepping, angling, weight distribution and body positioning

and unclear division of labour. In the years of Yung Cheng, Cheung Ng of Wu Pak, also known as Tan-Sau Ng, brought his skills to Fatshan and organised the Hung Fa Wui Koon (now the Chinese Artist Association). From there, Cantonese opera made great progress.

The book also records:

Besides being very accomplished in Chinese opera,

Cheung Ng was especially proficient in martial arts. His tan sau was peerless throughout the martial arts world.

Another piece of information appears on page 631, Volume III of the book *A History of Chinese Opera*, by Mang Yiu, first published by Chuen Kay Literature Publishers in 1968.

For some reason, Cheung Ng could not stay on in the

'Trapping the spear'

Kau dau/Cham dao

capital, so he fled and took refuge in Fatshan. This was during the reign of Yung Cheng. This man, nicknamed Tan-Sau Ng, was a character 'unsurpassed in literary and military skills, and excellent in music and drama'. He was especially proficient in the techniques of Siu Lim. After settling down in Fatshan, he passed on his knowledge in traditional opera and martial arts to the Hung Suen (Red Boat) followers, and established the Hung Fa Wui Koon in Fatshan. Today, Cantonese opera groups revere him as Jo-Si (Founding Master), and refer to him as Master Cheung. From the two passages above we learn: Cheung Ng, also known as Tan-Sau Ng, not only excelled in martial arts, but actually taught the techniques himself. He was dubbed 'Tan-Sau Ng' because of his 'tan sau . . . peerless throughout the martial arts world.'

Comparing the legend of Yim Wing Chun with the information on Tan-Sau Ng, I consider the latter more acceptable in our examination of

Lap dao/Cham dao

Tan dao/Cham dao

Wing Chun's origins. The reasons are as follows:

1) Cheung Ng brought his skills to Fatshan during the reign of Yung Cheng. This was forty to fifty years before the great fire of Siu Lam during the reign of Kin Lung (1736–1795). It was almost a hundred years before the legend of Yim Wing Chun, which fell within the Ham Fung (1851–1861) and Dao Kwong (1821–1850) years.

2) Tan sau is a technique unique to Wing Chun. Cheung Ng was famous for his tan sau. Cheung Ng actually taught martial arts in Fatshan Hung Suen (Red Boat). And Fatshan was the breeding ground of Wing Chun.

3) Some years ago, my Kung Fu clansman Pang Kam Fat told me that the Wing Chun stance is best used on boats for stability. Looking further, the various sets of martial arts strokes and practice areas are closely related to practice on narrow boats.

Gang dao

Yat dao

4) Before the skills were handed down to Leung Jan, the people connected, including Leung Lan Kwai, 'Painted Face Kam', Wong Wah Bo and Leung Yee Tei, all belonged to the Hung Suen (Red Boat).

Yet it is very difficult to verify the origin of Wing Chun with so little material about Cheung Ng. So, before we find more information and proof, we can perhaps make the following assumptions:

During the reign of Yung Cheng, Wu Pak actor Cheung Ng, also known as Tan-Sau Ng, for some reason fled the capital and went to Fatshan. He organised the Hung Fa Wui Koon at Tai Kay Mei, Fatshan. Apart from teaching traditional operas, he also taught the techniques of martial arts, and was called Master Cheung. The martial arts skills he taught already had the principles and techniques of Wing Chun martial arts.

Mun dao

Kup dao

Perhaps they can be called incomplete or inadequately practised Wing Chun martial arts. A hundred years passed in dissemination (mainly in Hung Suen) and development. Much effort was made by Yim Wing Chun, Leung Bok Chau, Wong Wah Bo, Leung Yee Tei and others. Wing Chun became a complete and mature set of martial arts, which spread and flourished under Leung Jan.

The above assumption eliminates the mythical padding to Wing Chun, and presents an orderly progress of events. It also provides a trail which can be followed by people interested in the history of Wing Chun.

Double lan dao

Fak dao/Lan dao

MY FATHER, GRANDMASTER YIP MAN

My father passed away on 1st December, 1972. Of course throughout the lifetime of Grandmaster Yip Man there have been many items of worth to remember him by. When you think in just twenty-two years (1950–1972), from there being no Wing Chun in Hong Kong, it has spread to cover the whole world, creating many respected martial artists as well as the cult hero Bruce Lee.

Regrettably, a lot of the remembrance is artificial. Much that has been written about Yip Man neglected his better points and failed to pass on his knowledge, so missing the opportunity to influence the rest of the world.

Most of the articles concentrate too much on describing how good Yip Man's Kung Fu was. This is a fact that cannot be denied, but it must be remembered that for the last twenty years of his life in Hong Kong, due to his well-controlled temperament, he was never in a situation where he needed to use his Kung Fu skill. The written accounts of Yip Man's prowess are really only the history of his younger days, and not at all the way Yip Man should be remembered.

The martial arts world is a very knowledgeable circle; if you can only talk about Kung Fu you will never be recognised as a master. Throughout the world today Yip Man is respected as one of the great grandmasters, and this reflects the real person.

There have been articles that have exaggerated the status of many authors, maintaining that they were *the* favourite and closest students of Yip Man and therefore they were taught differently; in addition they lay claim to have been taught secret techniques (e.g. death touch or dim mak). This concerns me and I must clarify the situation.

Firstly, Yip Man was very serious about his professional ethics. He would treat each of his students the same, trying his best to teach them his knowledge and if they were hard-working they all became successful.

Therefore I hope that in future there will be no writing about Yip Man purely to promote the author, which in the process destroys the true image of their beloved teacher.

Secondly, since as today we live in a realistic society, not the fantasy of novels, the truth is that in Kung Fu there are no secret techniques or secret scripts. Anyone who talks in terms of secret techniques or secret scripts does not understand what real Kung Fu is about.

Yip Man, 1894-1972

Anyone who thought that Yip Man was only good at the practical aspects of Kung Fu did not understand him. In reality, more important than his Kung Fu was his ability to teach people his Kung Fu.

When Yip Man began teaching in Hong Kong in the 50s he appreciated that to be a good Kung Fu instructor it is not enough to have excellent Kung Fu; it is essential that the instructor knows how to teach students. Yip Man understood that the aim of the majority of students was to actually learn the Kung Fu from the teacher so they could keep it for themselves. However, up to now a lot of instructors have spent too much time and effort boasting about their Kung Fu in front of their students and in the media, rather than using that time to improve their teaching method.

Although Yip Man did not have an official education in teacher training, he realised the importance of a syllabus in a progressive teaching method during the learning process of a student. The first thing Yip Man did when he began teaching to a syllabus was to abandon all the complicated names such as pa kua or the five elements (metal, wood, water, etc.) and change the language to the modern form, making it easier for the students to understand.

Yip Man also abandoned the use of key words or phrases (e.g. 'strike comes at you, bridge on top of arm') – not that the knowledge was lost since they were translated into practical exercises so that the students no longer had to recite key words that had no real value.

In 1987 I invited all of Yip Man's students who were teaching, as well as those in Fatshan, to a meeting in a Hong Kong restaurant. We discussed our Kung Fu and its different forms. Yip Man's third student in Fatshan said that the Wing Chun in Hong Kong was missing a lot of techniques. For example, in Chum Kiu there was no knowledge of the five element footwork. He then demonstrated, we talked, and he found out that the Kung Fu taught in Fatshan and that being taught in Hong Kong were the same, the only difference being that those mysterious key words were missing.

A lot of people have said that Yip Man changed his Kung Fu. I talked many times with my father on this point, and he said, 'With Kung Fu, the simpler, the better. Grandmaster Leung Jan's last words were, "I spent the whole of my life trying to make Wing Chun simpler, but I was not successful". To allow the students to learn more systematically I rearranged and tidied up some techniques.' Therefore Yip Man never changed the traditional forms, he only cut out the unnecessary parts. The reason being to make it easier for the students to accept the forms.

Yip Man knew that Chi Sau is the most important part of Wing Chun; Chi Sau is the intelligence of Wing Chun, its genius. Therefore he would concentrate a lot on Chi Sau. During the whole learning process, Chi Sau will make up almost 90 per cent of the input to a student's understanding of Wing Chun.

Yip Man's teaching method was to teach according to every student's personality, profession, education and body build, etc. He would study all these aspects then set up a systematic training method for each student.

Yip Man was gifted with the ability of good observation and an excellent memory. He only needed to have a 10–15-minute chat to get a complete picture which he would also never forget. I asked my father about the relationship between professional and educational backgrounds. His answer: 'Very important. If for example I was going to teach a student who was a professional hairdresser, it would be difficult for them to keep their elbows in; therefore you have to think of a different training method or find another technique to compensate. Alternatively if you have a student who has a heavy manual job or has studied a hard style of Kung Fu then to teach him to relax will be very difficult and you will have to teach him patiently. When teaching students who are well educated you only have to

Yip Chun attending his father's shrine, Hong Kong, 1989

say, 'Between two people a straight line is the shortest distance' and those students will understand clearly, but when teaching a person with no educational background you will generally have to give a more practical example to make him understand.'

Yip Man was a very realistic person, and everything he taught had to be explained and illustrated; he would never exaggerate a technique, using practical examples to explain to his students. If he was teaching the use of wu sau position, he would not tell the student to put his hand higher or lower, more forward, etc., rather he would get the student to understand the use of wu sau through experimentation with different wu sau positions, allowing the student to see which positions were correct.

My father would say, 'The human being should use Kung Fu, it should never be that Kung Fu uses the human being.'

These were words often used by Yip Man when teaching students Kung Fu, the meaning being that you must apply your Kung Fu freely, flexibly and never restrict the area in which you use a single technique.

There was one occasion when Sifu Lok Yiu and Sifu Wong Shun Leong were discussing Kung Fu and they had a difference of opinion on a particular technique, so they both went before Grandmaster Yip Man. The technique in question was the tan sau in the third part of Siu Lim Tao. Sifu Wong felt that the tan sau should come out facing palm down, the turn up on the way out. Sifu Lok believed that the tan sau should be used forward from holding the hand in a fist at the side of the body. The answer my father gave was that both of them were right. At the time this confused me a bit as I thought that Kung Fu should be absolute. How could two different ways be correct? Later I understood that, as tan sau is used to receive your opponent's straight punch from the indoor and that it must be done in the shortest time, therefore tan sau can come out from wherever the hands are positioned.

There are thousands of examples of my father's teaching methods; this has only been an insight to a small part.

CHI SAU

I must begin by saying that theory alone is totally useless. It doesn't matter how good your theory (or philosophy) is, if you don't put it into practice it will be of no use to you. However, a sound theoretical base can help you achieve much better results through your practice and will make it easier for you to improve.

Therefore, it is necessary to discuss some aspects of the theory – and one aspect in particular: Chi Sau. This is because, in Wing Chun, Chi Sau is a very important aspect. When learning or practising Wing Chun one's ability is not determined by how well one does the forms (hand techniques) but by how well one does Chi Sau.

When playing Chi Sau, fellow students of Wing Chun ask each other: 'How's your Chi Sau?' We do not use the forms or wooden dummy technique for comparison of skill but we do use Chi Sau. This is because we are all learning Wing Chun, and by playing with a few Chi Sau techniques one can judge one's Wing Chun ability. So, in my Kung Fu teaching experience, Chi Sau is the most important factor.

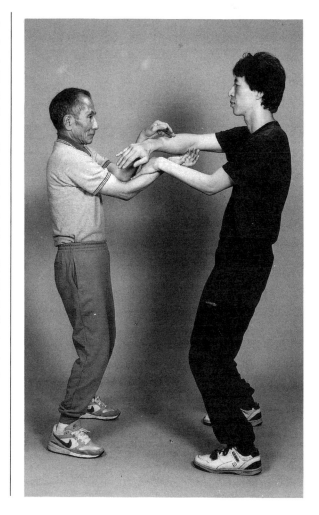

Yip Chun and Samuel Kwok

What is Chi Sau?

It can be said that Wing Chun Chi Sau practice is a unique training process or exercise because, no matter what your style of Kung Fu, there is nothing comparable to it in its completeness.

Certainly, Tai Chi has pushing hands, but its version can be said to be totally different from Wing Chun Chi Sau, because when they push hands only one particular energy is being applied. Therefore, I feel that the Tai Chi pushing hand technique is not very complete.

Recently, in England, there was a girl named Imelda who also won a Tai Chi pushing hand championship. Although she had learned a bit of Tai Chi before, she maintained that she had applied the Wing Chun energy principles to win the championship. Therefore, even now, there is hardly one Kung Fu style that has such a complete exercise as Chi Sau in Wing Chun.

What is so special about Chi Sau?

Well, it is its own training exercise. First of all, you have to understand that sticking hands is not the same as forms or free fighting, and you must remember that Chi Sau is not a set of movements. Biu Tze, wooden dummy techniques, knife, etc., can be regarded as forms, but Chi Sau cannot since it has no fixed movement.

Siu Lim Tao, Chum Kiu and Biu Tze all have fixed movements and positions. Even after practising them a hundred times, they still remain the same. When playing Chi Sau, however, there may be some similarity at the beginning, but after a few techniques, nothing will be repeated exactly as you continue to play.

Nor is Chi Sau like free fighting. The point of free fighting is the contest, the deciding of a winner and a loser. The ultimate aim is to knock down your opponent!

Chi Sau is, on the other hand, an exercise, a training process, and from it one should learn something – and I don't mean how to knock

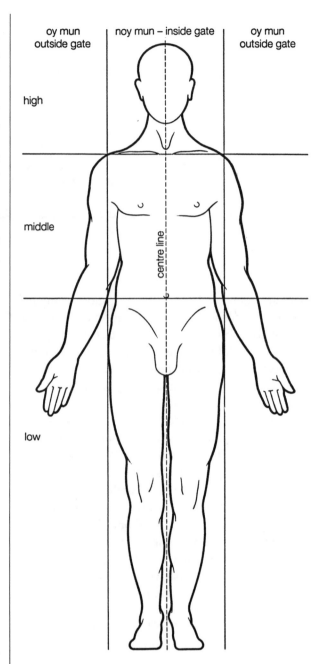

down one's opponent. Chi Sau should be regarded as a bridge between forms and free fighting. Once you have learned the forms it is necessary to use the Chi Sau process to 'bridge' you to the free fighting stage. Chi Sau is a bridge which links the forms and hand technique to the free fighting reality.

If there were no Chi Sau process and one applied the forms in free fighting with someone, would they work?
Yes. As a matter of fact you can free fight with someone else even without having learned any Kung Fu (or forms). But, once you have learned the forms and hand techniques, then you would wish to know how to apply them all in free fighting.

If there were no Chi Sau process would you still be able to do that?
Yes, but it would take a very long time. That is to say, you need to have a lot of fights to enable you to learn how to apply the techniques in free fighting. In the process of having a lot of fights, there would be a big price to pay. One price would be the possibility of serious injury. This risk would continue until you had learned how to deal with free fighting.

Therefore, Wing Chun introduces Chi Sau in the hope that you can learn all the necessary techniques from it without paying such a price. And the fact that we are all learning the techniques from Chi Sau together, and we are all fellow students and Kung Fu brothers makes this possible. For example, elbow strikes and finger thrusting to the eyes are eliminated in club practice to avoid injury. The aim is that in a real free fighting situation the price you have to pay for success will be less. This is the function of Chi Sau.

Once you have learned all the forms and hand techniques you must use them in Chi Sau so that you can explore them for yourself. Then, you can apply these techniques in free fighting. This is the 'bridging' function of Chi Sau. Once you have learned the techniques through Chi Sau, you can deal with any fighting situation.

What can I learn from Chi Sau exercise and what can I gain from it?
Most people agree, and I have said many times: Wing Chun is a practical system and doesn't look pretty. So what are its benefits? There are two main ones, and they are acquired through the practice of Chi Sau:

- It gives you a healthy body and protection against illness.
- It works when you use it.

Let's consider the health factor first. There are a lot of people teaching Wing Chun and most of them neglect the health issue. How can one maintain a healthy body while learning Wing Chun? Perhaps I can best answer this by giving some information about myself.

I was born in 1924 but, despite my advanced years, I am still in good health. I play Chi Sau with every one of my students for a couple of hours without any problem. As for walking, I'm sure that some of you may not be able to catch up with me. When I walk with friends from Sai Kung to Sha Tin, passing through a few mountain ranges, it takes about five hours and I can still manage it.

How can I manage this at my age? Sometimes I do ask myself a similar question. In theory, my lifestyle is not very regular. I sometimes read a book until 3 or 4 a.m. and may even not sleep at all. Sometimes I go to bed late and at others I go to bed very early. Sometimes I can't sleep at nights so I get up and play game machines or occupy myself in some other way. All in all, my lifestyle is not normal. Sometimes I eat a lot, sometimes a little bit and sometimes I don't eat at all.

It's well known that although I don't drink at all I'm quite into pipe smoking. So, how is it that I have such a healthy body? I have given this much thought, and reckon that it is mainly due to learning Wing Chun.

This may sound unfounded or illogical to many people, but I have done a lot of research about health in relation to Kung Fu. For example, when a person is feeling ill it is of course necessary to treat the illness. In this world there are two basic ways of treating illnesses. One is to confront the disease (as is done in the West); that is to say that after you have contracted a certain illness and the doctor has diagnosed it, then the doctor prescribes some medicine or treatment to defeat the illness and the patient then recovers. So, this is a 'fight against' method to treat the illness.

The other method is the natural way. In our bodies there are some antibodies which fight against invading foreign bodies. As a matter of fact, every living thing has such capabilities whether it's an animal or a plant, but since we human beings are living in a busy modern world, our internal defence capability (or immune system) is declining gradually, due to air pollution, junk food, environmental pollution, noise, etc., and also emotional stress. This is not obvious when you are young, but it becomes more apparent as you grow older.

The noxious influences I've mentioned affect our bodies directly and indirectly, causing a lot of harm. Gradually your body becomes less healthy, less robust. And that is when it becomes very easy to contract an illness. In Chinese medicine, the body would now be described as weak, but it is still possible to find a way to get the body strength back to normal so that its defence mechanism can perform its function and fight against foreign invaders. In Chinese medicine there are two ways to get the body strength back to normal:

1) By taking medicine – normally an expensive

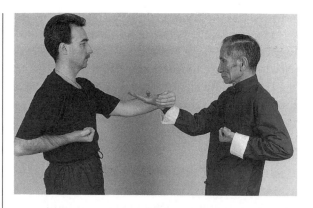

Dan Chi Sau – single sticking hand exercise. A drill to teach to react to a movement and to flow from attack into defence or vice versa.
  Above: Opponent – fook sau, YC – tan sau

As above – to show lack of footwork and/or turning of body

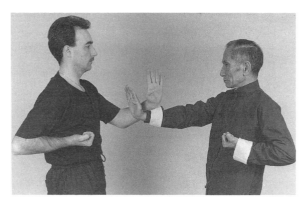

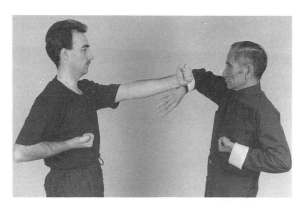

YC strikes with vertical palm, his opponent parries with jum sau

The opponent then strikes with yat chi kuen (single punch). YC counters with bong sau

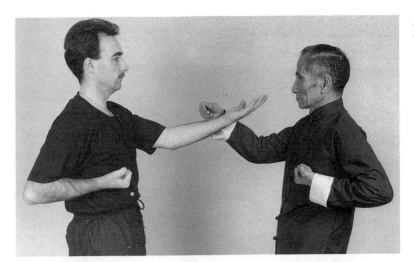

As on previous page, each with opposite techniques

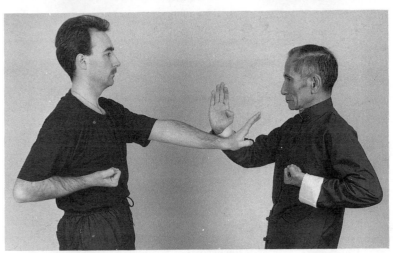

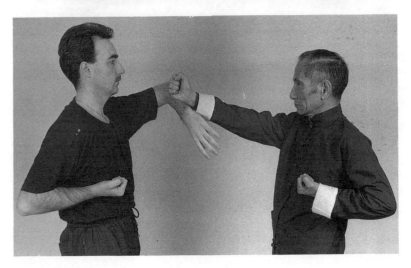

type, such as ginseng. Even if you can afford such medicine there are still drawbacks, because the more of it you take, the larger the quantity needed to have an effect. It is possible to gradually develop a dependence which can lead to addiction.
2) By doing exercise or training to get your body back to a healthy state. As a matter of fact there are a lot of exercises which can do this. One obvious one is Qigong.

Recently a lot of people have got into Qigong practice. Its main purpose is to increase the body's defence mechanism so it can effectively combat illness and disease.

Some people like to idolise or deify Qigong and sometimes they claim that, while in the process of doing it, they can foresee the future, that they can use the 'Qi' energy to heal the sick, etc. But we are going to ignore these sort of claims.

In China, apart from Qigong, there are lots of other training methods, like morning exercises, Tai Chi and some other Kung Fu forms, keep-fit exercise or even just swinging your arms and shaking your legs. You can see a lot of people in the early hours of the morning, in parks or on the top of hills, doing some form of morning exercise. These people are mainly old people who have found that physical culture improves their lives.

But, no matter which method you use, if you want to have a healthy body, you must be aware that in the process of exercising your mind must be relaxed and focused only on the activity in question. If you cannot achieve this it is equivalent to not doing any exercise at all and your body's defence mechanism will not improve significantly. It is, of course, very difficult to both relax your mind and concentrate it on the exercise completely.

What types of Qigong are there?
There are two types:

- Taoist Qigong, which emphasises calm and peacefulness.
- Buddhist Qigong, which emphasises stability and tranquility.

So, what is meant by these states of peacefulness and stability?
They refer to the state of mind already mentioned, in which you just relax your brain completely and concentrate on the activity. This is extremely difficult to do, especially in today's society.

A lot of Qigong teachers realise that their students find it difficult to achieve the calmness or stability state required. To help them, a sort of 'hypnotic' method has been devised. Let me give an example. In a normal standing type of Qigong, the body is relaxed and the hands hold an imaginary ball in front of the body. This 'ball' must be held firmly and not released. If the hands become loose the 'ball' will drop to the floor. Once it is on the ground all the air inside the 'ball' is released and this indicates that you are failing to learn Qigong.

Once your mind is concentrating on holding the 'ball' you won't be thinking about anything else. This method has something of a hypnotic effect, and clears the mind of the constant everyday thoughts of bills, business deals and meetings, etc. Your mind is still thinking, but only about the 'ball'.

There are some methods that are being used with an increased level of hypnosis to calm people down completely, but these are not a good idea and in a few cases the opposite effect is achieved. Such practices are regularly exposed in the press and on TV in Hong Kong and China; many claims by so-called masters of Qigong have been refuted and they have been accused of attempting to deceive the public.

Nevertheless, for the majority of us, it is difficult to concentrate on exercise and keep the mind calm. But there is one method that could guarantee that you will not think of anything

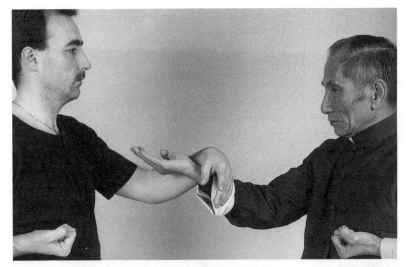

Opponent and YC single sticking hand position (opponent fook sau, YC tan sau). YC demonstrates step-by-step change from inside gate to outside gate. This occurs during the repeated rolling process. The opponent commences roll to bong sau

As opponent's elbow rolls up, YC feels movement and . . .

else once you have started doing it.

Which method is that?

Chi Sau.

Nowadays many people are familiar with or have practised Chi Sau. Well, perhaps some of these people think of something while playing Chi Sau. If they do you can be sure they find themselves getting hit quite frequently by their opponents. That is the risk of not concentrating on the exercise and so, in recent years in particular, I have found I am able to concentrate my mind on Chi Sau only. Once you've started playing Chi Sau you should definitely not think of anything else. Of course, there are a lot of sports that do need concentration but they don't necessarily have Chi Sau elements. Some other sports are quite energetic, like a game of football or a round of boxing – you wouldn't dare let your concentration lapse. But, absorbing as they are,

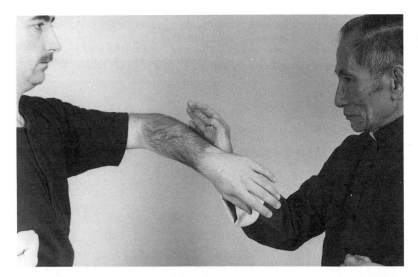

. . . commences huen sau to roll wrist over whilst controlling opponent's wrist

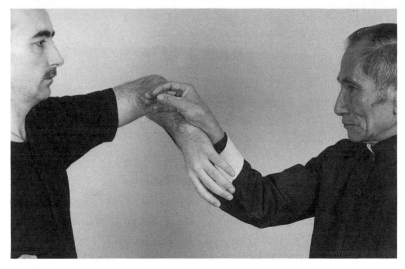

YC rolls over opponent bong sau, controlling with both wrist and elbow

do these have the same relaxation value as Wing Chun Chi Sau? This, incidentally, leads us on to another point: it is necessary to have a relaxing environment in which to play sports, to allow people to concentrate on the sport.

Chi Sau can be compared to the best methods of body training exercise; it is a good form of exercise for the body, maintaining health, and developing the skills and intelligence of an individual. These benefits form a unique part of Chi Sau, and I firmly believe that I owe my current good health to the practice of the exercise.

I said that Chi Sau's other great value is that it works when you use it. To explain this I need to draw your attention to the techniques used in free fighting, that is, the martial aspect. Four particular areas need to be developed:

- positioning
- knowledge of energy use

- sensitivity and reflexes
- hand techniques

These four things I have always emphasised, and perhaps they are not new to you. I intend to deal with each one in turn, but, as a matter of fact, these four skills should be executed at the same time in free fighting, and cannot be performed separately. We cannot just talk about hand techniques on their own. This is because often, when you are using hand techniques, you also need to incorporate sensitivity and reflexes, the correct use of energy and proper positioning. And then, sensitivity and reflexes are meaningless on their own because they will only show up when you perform a hand technique. The correct use of energy still requires the joint use of hand techniques and positioning. And with positioning you still need hand techniques, sensitivity and reflexes, and so on as mentioned above. So, when you are involved in free fighting, these four things fit together as one integrated action. In fact, if you can master and integrate these four things, you can easily deal with any situation under most circumstances.

But we still need to break this action down into its component parts so that everybody can understand what they are.

On many occasions in seminars I have held people have asked me how I would deal with someone hitting me in a certain way. I find I can answer these questions easily.

But afterwards, I gave it a bit of thought; I have never had a fight in my life, apart from a few half-forgotten and meaningless childhood scraps, but when people ask me these things, I can answer them back quite easily. Why is that?

I think the answer is that I have played a lot of Chi Sau; and in my thirty-odd years' experience of this aspect of Wing Chun, the four points listed above are paramount – good hand techniques, good sensitivity and reflexes, knowledge of energy use and good positioning.

If you only practise against a punch that comes

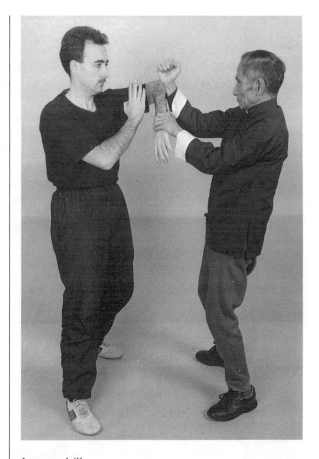

Lap sau drill
Opponent deflects YC punch with turn and bong sau

Lap sau application technique
On guard

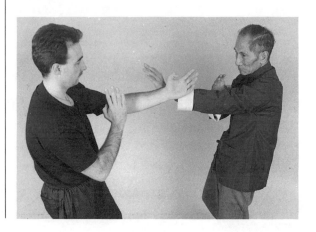

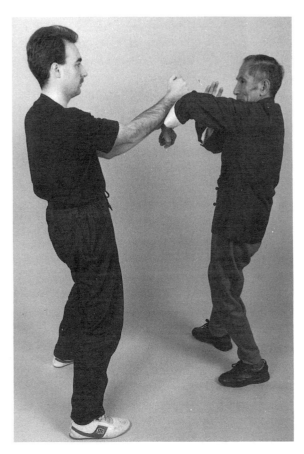

Opponent counters with a punch

YC feels the strike and begins to turn away, lifting his left elbow

YC lap sau to the opponent's leading arm, and feeds up the centre line. The opponent deflects with tan sau

YC receives the tan sau and instantly converts to left lap sau, then passes to gum sau (pinning hand) to pin and trap, leaving the right hand free to strike

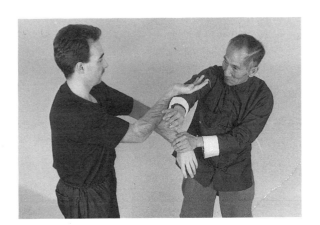

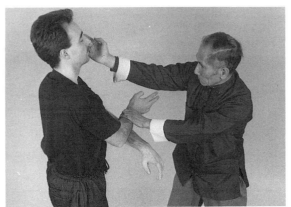

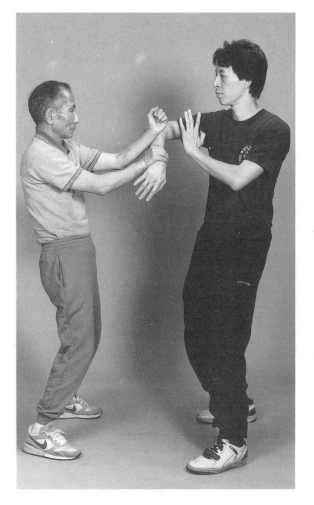 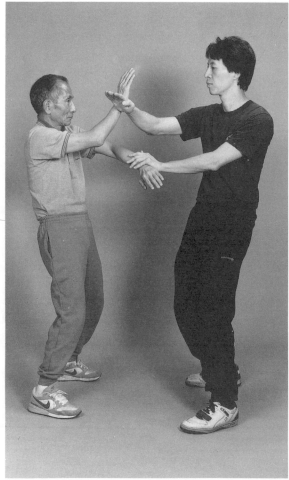

Lap sau technique showing deflection and turning

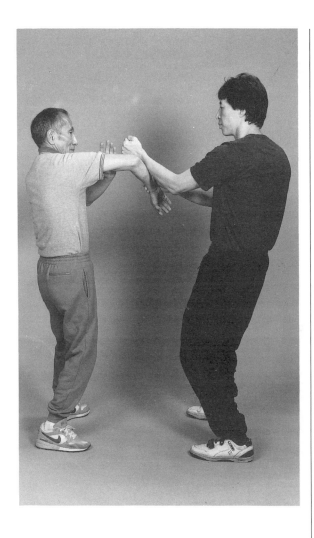

one way, how will you deal with a punch that comes another way? Won't you be totally lost? You should learn a method so that no matter how someone tries to hit you, you are still able to deal with it in a natural manner. The method is made up of these four things and, as I mentioned before, they should be executed together to make the movement effective.

Out of these four things, the easiest to learn is hand techniques – and it is also the least important. This judgement is based on my Kung Fu teaching experience. I play Chi Sau with a class every day for two hours. Within that time I will concentrate on one individual after another and the rest of the class can observe the hand techniques. Naturally, as time goes on, people learn to pick up my hand techniques; this you can tell just by looking at my students. And, clearly, it is easier to learn a technique that can be observed.

If you do a lap sau with your hand then your opponent will deal with it as shown in the photo. It may take him some time to learn how to counter your move but eventually he will learn it – because he will be able to see it better and better.

But the other three skills cannot be seen. Can you see sensitivity and reflexes? No. Can you see how energy is being used? Certainly not. Not even by standing next to that person.

When playing Chi Sau, if you pay attention you will notice that you can feel what my energy is like but you cannot see it. Positioning cannot be seen either. And, of course, a technique made up of a fixed set of movements is easier to learn than one that is not. It is easy, for example, to learn boxing moves, and if one session is not long enough then have two or maybe three. But Chi Sau is more difficult to learn because it is not a fixed set of movements in the same way.

You may know about sensitivity and reflexes but how can you *see* my sensitivity and reflexes? 'Wow, that was fast!' you might say as I execute a move. Basically speaking, the movement has included sensitivity, reflexes and good position-

Changes within lap sau drill

Opponent lap sau to YC arm and strikes. YC turns with bong sau to deflect the strike

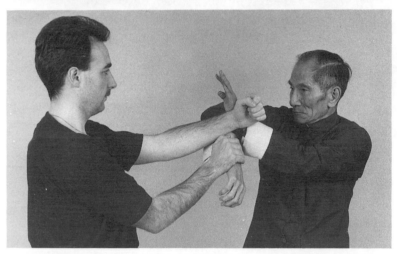

YC instantly counters with lap sau to opponent strike

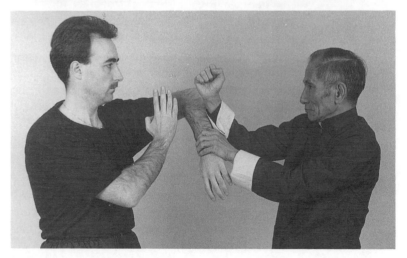

The opponent releases his contact on YC bong sau and turns to deflect the strike with bong sau

He attempts to lap sau YC with his bong sau arm

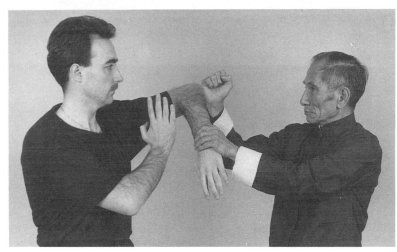

YC feels the energy change and counters his opponent with lap sau and strike. The opponent deflects with bong sau and turn, and so the drill exchange continues

ing. When a punch comes I already know what my opponent is up to and counter it very quickly. I combine hand techniques with good positioning, correct energy use and sensitivity and reflexes.

How do you learn sensitivity and reflexes if you can't see them? And if you can't see them won't it be a waste of time trying to learn them?

Sensitivity and reflexes can be acquired even though they can't be seen and are difficult to learn. This is because, within the process of Chi Sau, you will naturally develop a good sensitivity and reflexes as you get familiar with the exer-

43

Changes within lap sau drill
On guard position, i.e. neutral
advantage

YC lap sau to his opponent's leading
arm. The opponent converts to bong
sau and turns to deflect strike

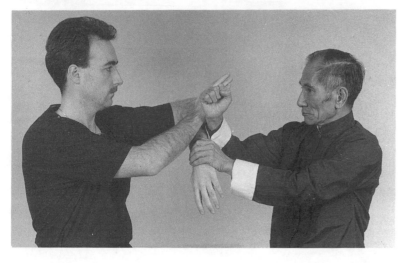

The opponent feeds wu sau up their
jic seen (centre line) to lap sau YC
punch

YC feels the contact at his wrist and counters with lap sau with his punch arm. Lifting his left elbow into bong sau to additionally control his opponent's right arm

Once YC lap sau begins to deflect his opponent's right arm, YC changes his left hand in to a punch

The opponent feels YC lap sau and strike and turns to deflect with bong sau, and so the drill continues

cise. This is because if you have no sensitivity or reflexes then it is quite easy for your opponent to hit you – so you will develop these skills out of an instinct for self-preservation. Clearly, then, it is not a waste of time to learn sensitivity and reflexes. They can be acquired so long as you keep playing Chi Sau. Therefore, there is no rush or panic to learn these things.

Let's turn now to energy, which is considered the most important of the four areas. Energy should be looked at from various angles. The most important point is that you should know how to conserve energy. A lot of times I use the money in your pocket as a comparison. Let's say you have a lot of money and I have only a little, but you keep spending unwisely. As a result, when you are in need of money there is not a lot, or nothing, left. When it comes to me, OK, perhaps I have little money but I know exactly how much I have got. And because I know how much I have got I will not waste it and will not spend it on unnecessary things. When there is no need to spend it I won't. Only when there is a need do I spend it. Therefore, at any time, I usually have money to spend. Energy is just the same. If you are relying on being young and energetic, you may have a lot of strength, but at the end there is always a limitation to the amount of energy at your disposal.

Humans do have limitations. The young and

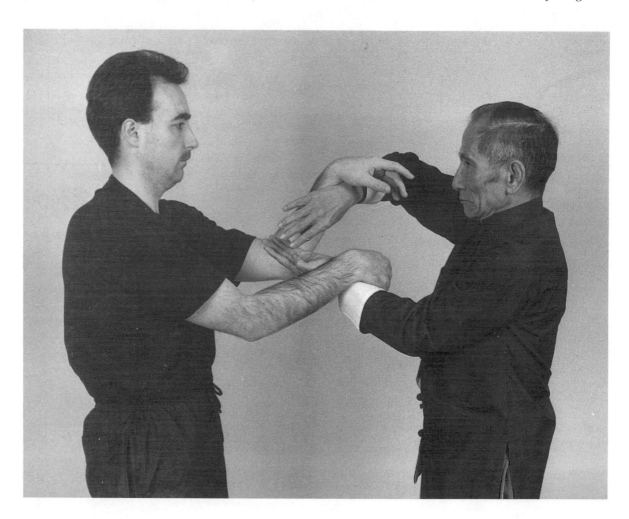

strong may believe they can expend energy whenever they wish, but there may be a time when it runs out just when you need it. If you conserve energy and don't waste it on everything you will always have the energy whenever you want to use it.

In combat, those who have a lot of experience will deliberately make you waste your energy until you have not much left, and then they can take their time to hit you back. So the first lesson is: conserve your energy.

The second concerns the use of energy. If one knows how to use energy and uses it in the right position and direction then the results will be good.

Seung Chi Sau – double handed Chi Sau

This is not a fighting method. It's a game to develop sensitivity, reflex, positions and techniques. It teaches attack, defence, counter attack, and counter defence, continually shifting the odds from one to the other. When both arms are linked, you put yourselves in a position of trust.

Chi Sau stages:

1. Poon sau – rolling arms

2. Luk sau – rolling arms with the forward energy. Training for lut sau jic chung (hand lost thrust forward)

3. Jeung sau – changing from inside gate to outside gate or vice versa

4. Gor sau – free application of technique

Poon Sau – rolling arms

Position 1 – YC rolls with both hands on the inside gate i.e. right: bong sau, left: tan sau

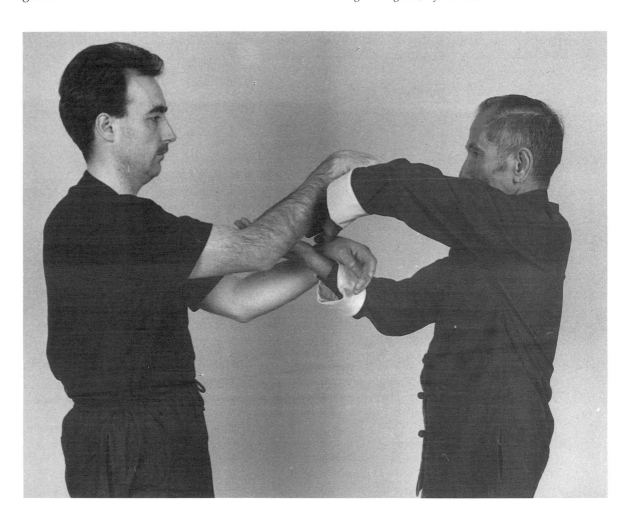

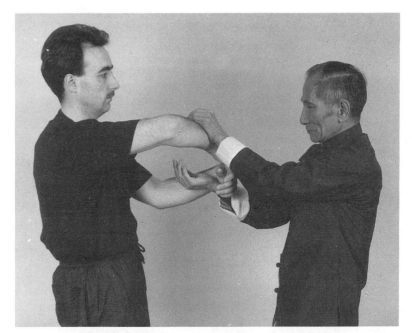

Position 2 – YC rolls with right hand on the inside gate and left hand on the outside gate, i.e. top picture R: tan sau, L: fook sau rolls to bottom picture R: bong sau, L: fook sau.

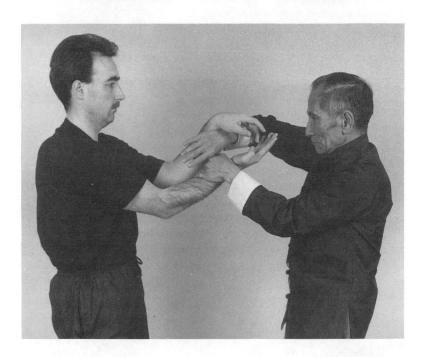

Position 3 – YC rolls with both hands on outside gate, i.e. both hands fook sau

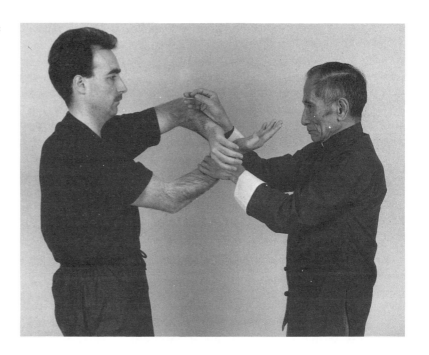

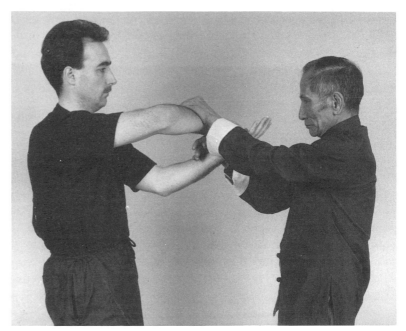

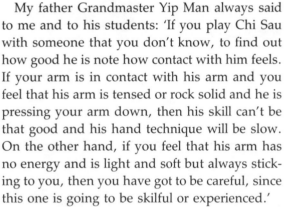

Wing Chun can easily be practised by both men and women safely

My father Grandmaster Yip Man always said to me and to his students: 'If you play Chi Sau with someone that you don't know, to find out how good he is note how contact with him feels. If your arm is in contact with his arm and you feel that his arm is tensed or rock solid and he is pressing your arm down, then his skill can't be that good and his hand technique will be slow. On the other hand, if you feel that his arm has no energy and is light and soft but always sticking to you, then you have got to be careful, since this one is going to be skilful or experienced.'

This is very true, as you will no doubt learn one day.

At the time that Yip Man said these things to me, it's possible that my Kung Fu wasn't that good. Only now am I beginning to understand what he meant. When we are rolling our hands, for example, do you think that energy should be used? Basically, there is no need to use energy at all and if you do it's wasted. And if you needlessly use energy to hold down your opponent, then you are wasting it. After a few rollings your opponent will take advantage of it and use it against you.

This brings us to a third point about energy: you can 'borrow' it from your opponent if he uses it at the wrong time. This is the use of energy at its highest level.

Correct use of energy will increase your Chi Sau ability by more than a half.

The last component of the method is proper positioning. This is the most difficult thing to acquire. There are many people who have been with me for quite some time and I have talked to them many times about hand techniques and pointed out there is not much difference between theirs and mine. This is because Wing Chun hasn't got many hand techniques, just tan, bong and fook. The question is how to use them? If someone is a bit better than you are then it is probably because their positioning is a bit better than yours. And this is usually the result of greater experience.

As a matter of fact, it is difficult for me to teach you how to be able to fully grasp good positioning. It should be experienced little by little within the process of Chi Sau. So, it is always down to playing more Chi Sau so that one will gain the experience to accomplish it.

What kind of Chi Sau attitude should you hold?
At the beginning, I said that Chi Sau is not the same as free fighting. Chi Sau is a learning process, and free fighting is about winning and losing, about counting blows and knock-downs.

Chi Sau is a 'honing' process.

Many people don't appreciate the difference between Chi Sau and free fighting. And if they get the two confused then there will be a lot of trouble, and they may be wanting to hit people all the time. If you think in that way then a lot of problems will arise; if you don't manage to hit someone and he manages to hit you instead, you will get angry. Then you will try even harder to hit him back and possibly even be heavy-handed. But using heavy hands to hit people is a very bad attitude towards Chi Sau. This is because we are all fellow students, Kung Fu brothers, and we all hope to learn something. When you use heavy hands to hit someone, he will feel the pain. And eventually neither of you will be happy about it. In such a situation, a person with a good temperament will think: 'Right, no more Chi Sau with you. I dread practising with you.' But a person with a poor temperament will try to hit you back no matter what. Then there will be an unpleasant scene. Having been a teacher of Wing Chun for a long time I have seen quite a few of these unpleasant scenes, although, of course, I always try to prevent them occurring.

There were two students, for instance, who both studied at the same university faculty together and graduated in the same year. They were the best of friends and came up to my place to learn Kung Fu. Both succeeded in this and their Kung Fu skills are very good.

But whilst they were playing Chi Sau as learners it somehow developed into an unpleasant situation. At the end, they were no longer friends. Wasn't that a pity? Originally the best of friends, they no longer want to see each other. One goes away as the other comes. They avoid each other. I tried to help a few times by talking to both of them but still couldn't do it. Isn't it a shame that because of abusing Chi Sau their friendship is at an end?

This was all due to an incorrect attitude towards Chi Sau. The major question you must ask yourself is: 'Why do I need to play Chi Sau?' Chi Sau is for learning. Since we are all learning something together, it makes no difference whether it's me hitting you or you hitting me. Why worry about it? If I am hit by a student whilst teaching – so what? If he manages to hit me then he has managed to hit me. I don't care at all. If he hits me by mistake I still don't care.

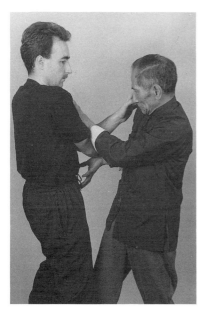

Left: Po pai – double pushing palms application. YC contacts with the fingers

Right: YC moves in to control before applying the po pai

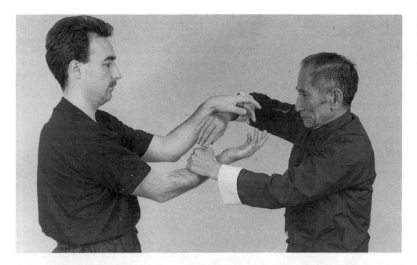

Applications of Chi Sau

These must be read and seen as continuous fluid movements.

The opponent and YC roll in Chi Sau

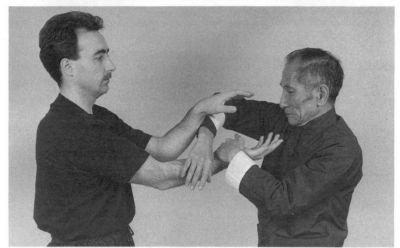

YC begins to feed him bong sau over the centre line

YC pak sau down on to his opponent tan sau with his right whilst feigning left strike

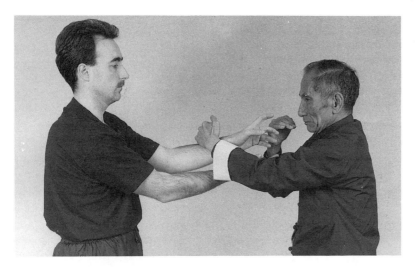

YC instantly turns to left feign into a pak sau to control both of his opponent's hands whilst freeing his right hand

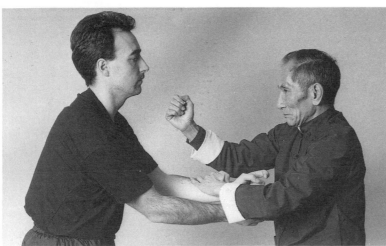

YC traps and controls both his opponent's hands with his left, leaving his right the choice of targets

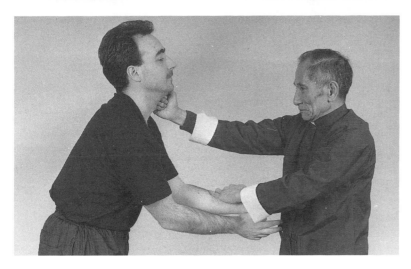

YC chooses to strike the throat – because it's there – and smiles inwardly. His opponent smiles outwardly with relief at YC control!

Applications of Chi Sau
As they roll in Chi Sau YC feeds his left over his right bong sau

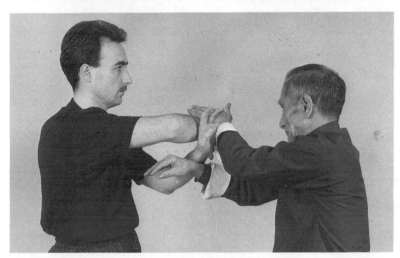

As the opponent's right arm rolls to bong sau, he feeds his left fook sau behind YC bong sau and lap sau

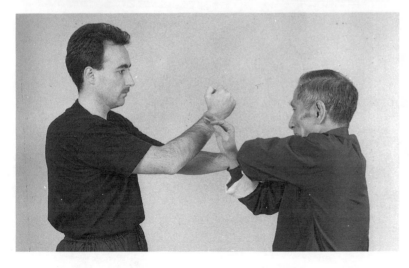

The opponent withdraws his right arm and punches to the centre line

There is no need to get angry about getting hit. In fact, when some other Kung Fu style practitioners pretend to be teaching Wing Chun, they are being foolish. This is because in playing Chi Sau at any time they could be hit by their student. This is not a surprise – split lips, bloody noses will always occur to the one who teaches Wing Chun, because he must practise Chi Sau with the students.

In the process of Chi Sau you should remain cool with your fellow students; only then will you be able to learn something. Then you will get through to hit me. But a student who hits too hard or retaliates too readily will end up having only his sifu (teacher) as a willing practice opponent. It is not possible to improve your Kung Fu skills in this way.

The first thing that you learn is how to hit, and the second thing that you learn is how to deal with an attack. You should learn about your opponent's hand techniques and see where his weaknesses are so that you can hit him back. But if you hit your opponent so he can feel the pain, you would then keep worrying about him hitting you back, and so not learn anything. To be able to learn something you must keep your temper under control. This is the correct attitude for learning Wing Chun and it must be observed.

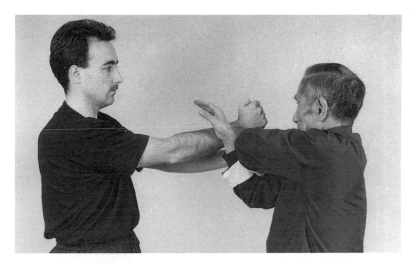

YC angles slightly and uses his gung lik (elbow energy) to destroy his opponent's attempted pin and feeds biu tze sau from beneath his bong sau

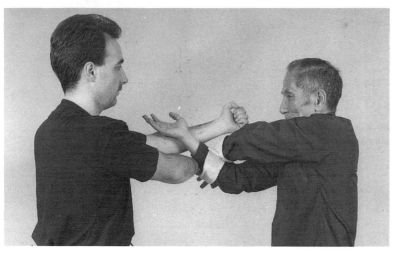

The opponent changes his light punch to a gum sau (pinning hand) and strikes with his left, but YC utilises his superior position and gung lik to maintain centre line control

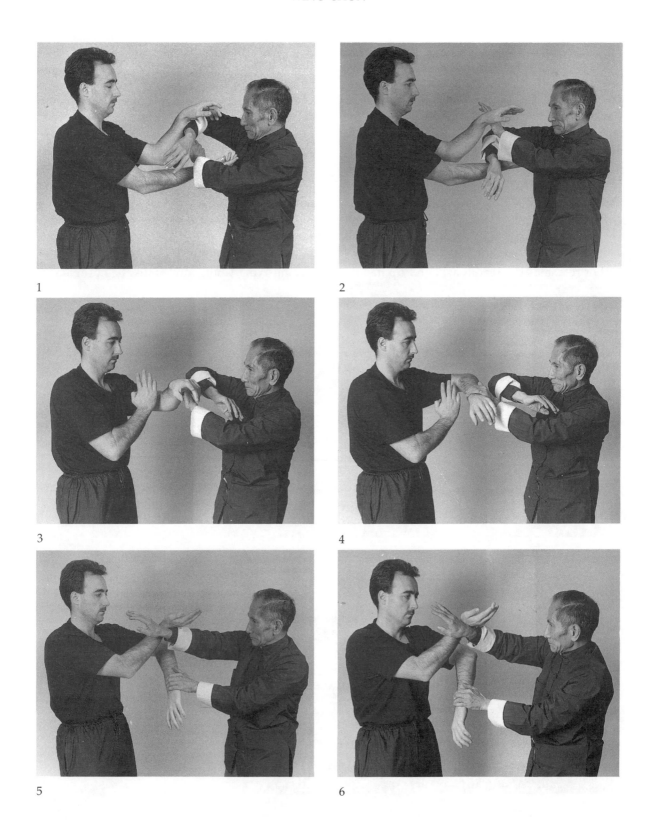

1

2

3

4

5

6

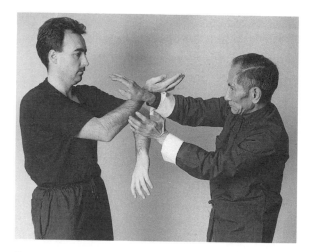

7

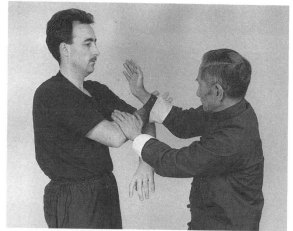

8

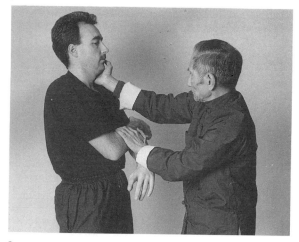

9

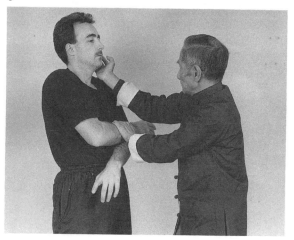

10

Applications of Chi Sau

1. As they roll in Chi Sau YC feeds his left over his right bong sau

2. YC swaps the contact arms, dropping his bong sau down whilst feeding his wu sau up

3. YC then lap sau his opponent's upper arm and goes to fak sau (whisking arm strike)

4. The opponent feels the lap sau and turns to deflect the potential strike with bong sau

5. YC feeds in a high strike so his opponent feeds his wu sau hand form to cover kwun sau (a high tan sau and low bong sau combination)

6. YC, as ever two moves ahead, reacts by converting his strike to a lap sau . . .

7. . . . pulling down his opponent tan sau over his bong sau and freeing YC's left hand . . .

8. . . . which YC converts to a gum sau (pinning hand) freeing his right hand

9. The gum sau pins both the opponent's arms and YC strikes a side palm to the throat with the heel of the palm

10. YC then rolls his thumb towards his opponent's left eye socket and thankfully stops

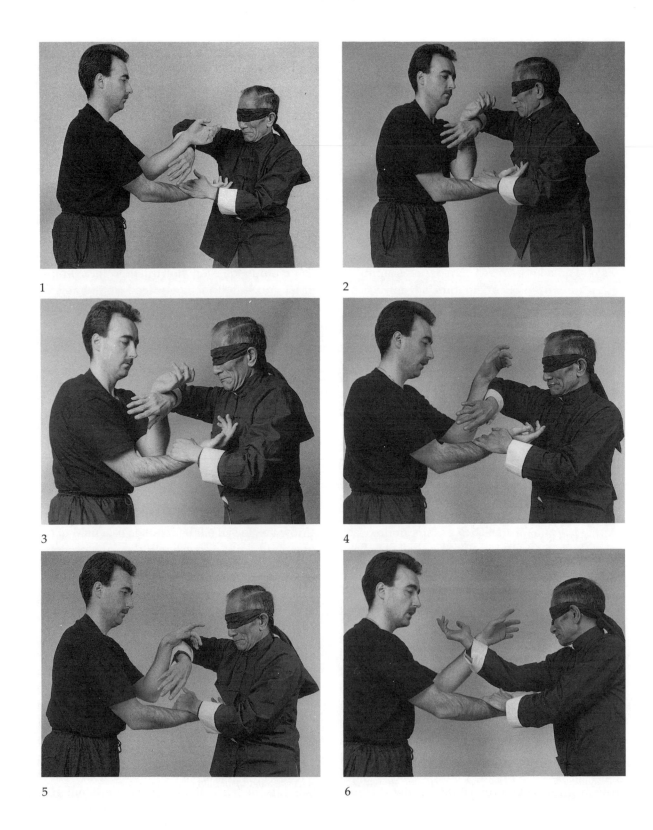

1

2

3

4

5

6

If I want to defend myself against someone attacking me in another Kung Fu style, should I deal with him differently in terms of hand techniques?

As far as hand techniques and hitting people are concerned, it's all the same; quite simply, your opponent intends to hit you and if you really have a grasp of the four components of the technique you can deal with any situation, even using your legs if necessary, especially if you are good at positioning and have well-developed sensitivity and reflexes. You don't need to worry about what hand techniques or Kung Fu style he is using – to hit you he must come towards his target. If all aspects of your technique are good and complete, your reaction will be natural and there will be no special need for any rehearsal beforehand. You should ask yourself whether you have a grasp of the four basics. Have you spent enough time on Chi Sau?

Does Wing Chun have leg techniques? If so, how do you practise them?

In Wing Chun dummy (wooden man) practice there are eight leg movements and under different circumstances each one is used. If your Chi Sau skill is good and you have a grasp of the four basic techniques you should be able to perform them.

You have mentioned early on that if you play a lot of Chi-Sau your technique and sensitivity will improve. Some people say this is to the detriment of developing leg skill.

If your positioning and reflexes are good then I don't see that there is going to be any problem at all. When you are practising on the dummy you will train your legs and they should be powerful after you have mastered the dummy form. I have never mentioned anything relating to the 'heavy' (being strong or powerful) side of things, only about hitting people a bit hard. Chi Sau is not about the hands or the legs being strong or powerful. If you want to train your punch, or your legs, you must put a lot of effort into it. To train your legs you must loosen up the leg muscles. To train your punches you must practise a lot of straight punching into the air.

7

Blindfolded chi sau. The highest level of sticking hands is to defend blindfolded. This training refines and hones the sensitivity.

1. YC tricks his opponent

2. YC presses his bong sau forward and presses his opponent down slightly to create a reaction

3. The opponent feels the pressure of the bong sau and dissolves the energy using seung lik (withdrawing the force) whilst using gung lik (elbow energy) to maintain the tan sau position

4. YC feels his opponent's gung lik and angles slightly to dissolve its effects, whilst using his bong sau elbow to control his opponent's fook sau

5. YC switches off his bong sau energy (seung lik) whilst still controlling his opponent tan sau

6. The opponent feels YC switch off his bong sau energy and pushes forward. YC instantly rolls from bong sau to tan sau and feeds up the centre line. His opponent's face tells of the realisation of the trick, as YC smiles to himself

7. YC closes in using left pak sau to control his opponent's left hand whilst YC left elbow controls his opponent's right arm. YC right strike is blocked by his opponent's throat!

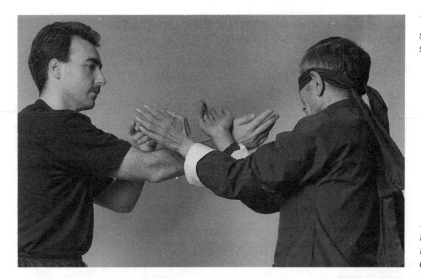

YC deflects the opponent's right strike. The opponent begins a left strike . . .

. . . which as soon as it is fed through is pinned and trapped. YC again introduces his free hand to his opponent's chin

A lot of people think that Wing Chun is a 'soft' style but to some others, a 'hard' style. I am not too sure whether the 'hard' style can take a blow from a 'soft' style and 'soft' style can take a blow from a 'hard' style . . .

You can certainly say it's possible that an opponent might withstand your blow and you might not withstand his. I don't think that Wing Chun is a 'soft' style Kung Fu but a 'hard' style Kung Fu. This is because when you are hitting someone you've got to use energy, in other words, force. Otherwise your opponent won't feel the pain and it will seem like just a scratch. I said that the only time when you use energy is when you need it – when dealing a blow, for example. There is no point in hitting your opponent with nothing behind the punch. The time taken for you to expend energy when hitting is very short. When you throw a punch it should be faster and more powerful than your opponent's. This is because the amount of time you spend on expending energy is very short – as long as it takes to punch – while your opponent is all tensed up and using energy all the time.

Have you ever practised your punches to see whether they are powerful enough to inflict pain or not?

All this is not about being powerful in Wing Chun, but about practising your punches so they

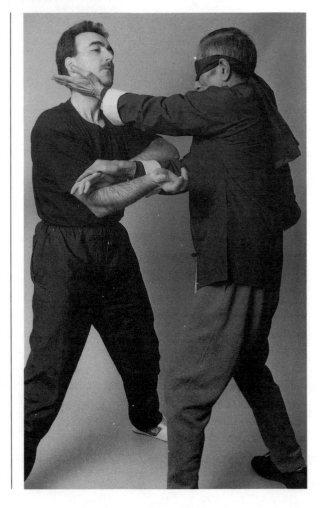

Chi Sau here being demonstrated to show the level of skill that may be obtained

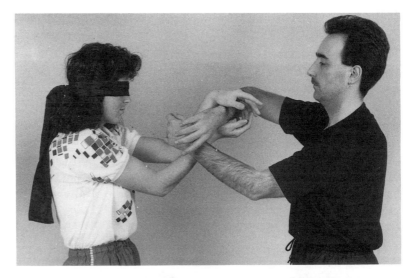

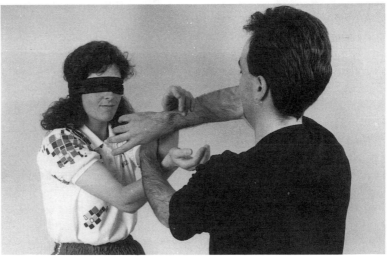

can be powerful. Whether you can take your opponent's punch or he can take your punch depends on your physical strength and self-defence ability. It has nothing to do with practising a 'soft' or a 'hard' Kung Fu style. You should not feel that Wing Chun is 'soft'. Wing Chun in fact is 'hard'. When a punch is landed it is solid as a rock. If the punch is soft when landed how can it inflict pain on the opponent? A soft punch is useless in combat.

Students who practise punches on wall bags and into the air a lot realise that these punches can be very powerful. If your opponent, from beginning to end, is tense and wasting energy, while you only use the energy when you need it, then your punches should be more powerful than his even though he may be stronger.

There is a lot of emphasis on the fact that the hands must be placed on the centre line, but I only have one centre line. Suppose my opponent has already occupied the centre line, should I retake or compete for the centre line, or should I move to another position to compensate for this disadvantage? I have sometimes felt that I and my opponent have occupied each other's centre lines.

There is no reason why you can't grasp hold of your own centre line and let your opponent occupy your centre line. You must be able to hold your centre line and then there is no way that an opponent can control your centre line.

It is possible to get your centre line and your opponent's centre line a bit mixed up. Your opponent will have a lot of difficulties in occupying your centre line, and he is not going to be so foolish as to try to do so. If he does he will be very passive or will have to do a lot of work. If he is having a real fight with you then he will get tired very quickly. If he tries to occupy your centre line and you move then he will have to go round again and try once more to occupy it. It is the same in Chi Sau.

As a matter of fact, the question should really be about the meridian line, which is the line that links up your centre line and your opponent's centre line. This is the line that should be taken. Whoever can get hold of the meridian line will have the advantage. To have a good positioning is all based on a good grasp of the meridian line rather than your centre line or your opponent's centre line.

When we are playing Chi Sau how do we use energy? By pushing each other, or in some other way?

Wing Chun says that you should use energy with a bit of thought. Be clever about it. This means knowing when to use it and when to conserve it. It also means knowing where to use it; in which position or angle will its use give you an advantage? If my hand is holding off your hand in such a way that my position is a bit better than yours, then I will contend with you. If the situation is reversed then I won't contend with you and will try to avoid you instead.

You will learn the right circumstances in which to expend energy through playing a lot of Chi Sau. Even though my opponent might be bigger and stronger than me and I am not as young as he is, if my positioning is better than his he still won't be able to contend with me.

What is the effect of being big and strong in Chi Sau?

It is always an advantage being big and strong and having a lot of strength even when relaxed. So people with a small build should be even more clever in the use of energy and should become more agile. Being agile might mean nothing more than taking a couple more steps and turning in a few more stances – it will allow you to avoid using strength against strength.

SIU LIM TAO
(THE FIRST FORM)

Siu Lim Tao, which is the fundamental training of Wing Chun and can be translated as 'the small idea', is broken into three parts. The first part is a build-up of energy. The opening moves, cross down and cross up, are used to define the centre line and are not blocking techniques; this goes back to the days before mirrors, when practitioners used to stick a pole in the garden, stand in front of it, cross down and up and align themselves with the pole to define their centre line.

This first third is performed with a lot of strength and tension in the arm, concentrating on fingertips, thumb, wrist, elbow, shoulder, and getting the correct tension. From here we go on to the second third, which is about using energy, focusing it into the end, the last six inches, which is the basis of Wing Chun.

This second part of Siu Lim Tao concerns the development of the proper use of power. Power is an arbitrary word for me. Ging is inner strength, a release of energy – Ging Lik, you catch it in a certain place of the body. There are two main branches of Kung Fu, 'hard' and 'soft'. 'Hard' is when you have to stiffen the hands, 'soft' is when you relax. In Wing Chun there is a refinement of energy, a mixture of the two. The reason why Wing Chun is a mixture of the two is determined by the punch.

When it is powerful, that is 'hard'; the use of the 'soft' depends on different cases. For example, when I punch you with a Wing Chun punch, before I reach you the fist is soft; once the fist contacts it is hard, so you don't stiffen the hand before it reaches the body; once it has made contact it returns to being soft. When it reaches the body it makes an explosive power on contact, concentrating the energy on the fist. Once it has contacted the hands relax as quickly as possible. It slows you down to stiffen your hands. At the beginning of the second part of Siu Lim Tao go slowly, slowly, relax, then go hard, then soon after relax. This principle is from all other forms. This theory of the principles of being hard and soft and the proper release of power is known as Ging Lik. I prefer the term inner strength much more than power. In the second part of Siu Lim Tao the use of the fighting power lasts a very short time because it is explosive. There is no real name for this movement.

The last third, practising the techniques, uses the energy that you have built up in the first third and learned how to use in the second third. This part of Siu Lim Tao should be done not too fast, but not too slow – tense, relax, tense, relax – all these techniques are to give you the correct position. This is very important in the early stages so you can focus on one spot and keep that spot precise. From the side view we can see the different aspects of the distance and off to the bud, the idea that the elbow should be a fixed distance from the body. You can also start to see where the energy is placed when the punch is made in the last six inches. Emphasis again is on slow and deliberate movements; only through slow and deliberate movements can you practise seriously.

Huen Sau

Siu Lim Tao (pronounced sue lim taw) translates as 'way of the little idea' or 'little idea form'.

It is the dictionary of Wing Chun. It is now definitive in so far as any applications, but contains the vital elements essential to energy and position training: the foundation of the system.

108 movements – 3 sections

Section 1 – slow dynamic tension exercise using antagonistic muscle groups of the biceps and triceps to develop the correct elbow energies.
Section 2 – a sequence of movements practising to relay and explode the movements, to train to use out the energies trained in Section 1.
Section 3 – Basic hand positions and techniques utilising the energies and relaxation of the first two sections.

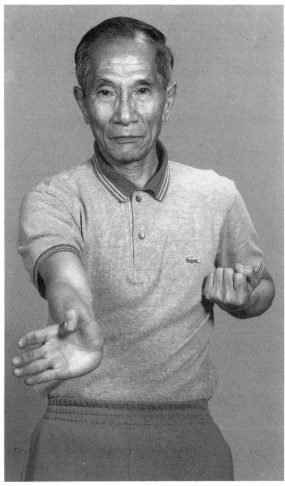

Huen sau

Low side palm

Section 2
Double lan sau

Double jum sao (sinking elbow)

Pak sau – slapping hand

Bong sau (wing arm)

Tan sau (palm up)

In a detailed description of the first form, the cross down technique defines the centre line, punch into the centre line and out, focus, circle, close and back. Left tan sau, hand over, slowly bring the hand, wrist first, then elbow follows into the centre line, push out steady and with strength so the elbow is one fist distance off the body. Huen sau into the wu sau position, go back, relax down, maintain the wrist in the centre line position, into the first fook sau, push out, bring elbow in, one fist distance off the body, huen sau into wu sau position and go back and relax. Down into the second fook sau, push out, bringing the elbow in, constant reminder that the elbow should be coming in, going back into the wu sau, relaxing down for the third time. The energy here should be in the wrist, fingertips, thumb, elbow, drawn back, pak, palm flat like huen sau, close, repeated on right hand side. Again tan sau into the centre, palm flat. The position of the hand is important, the height of tan sau, the wrist shouldn't be too low.

This movement can be done very slowly but with a lot of strength, a lot of tension, building up muscle power in the wrist, elbow and forearm. It can also be done relaxed for a longer time, concentrating on the idea of getting the elbow into the centre, focusing the wrist first and

Reverse palm strike

times in Wing Chun, through the nose, tongue pressed into the mouth. Breath in and out using the stomach. At all times when practising you should be aware of your stance and your other hand. When doing tan sau, huen sau, wu sau, fook sau, huen sau, movements, the other hand should be held back, horizontal, the fist pulled right back up against the chest; this also exer-

Cheung choy – battle punches. Basic centre line punches

then pushing out, using the elbow with a piston-like effect, so all the time the elbow is behind the wrist whenever it pushes out. From the side view you can see the precise position more clearly; this is very important, as is the use of energy in the last few inches. The huen sau movement should be done a lot slower, again for wrist and forearm strengthening. The tan sau should be approximately at throat level. In wu sau the fingers should be vertical and straight; draw back using the elbow, pushing the wrist out and bringing the elbow behind, so using energy to push out and pull back.

Breathing should be relaxed and natural at all

Gan sau – cutting down

cises the shoulder. Your stance is important; you should always hold position in your stance, you should not bounce. This is possibly the most important part of the Wing Chun system because if you don't practise the first third of Siu Lim Tao you will never develop proper energy to be effective in your techniques. The power in the hands is developed to be used in strikes and blocks.

The second third (also very important) concerns the use of energy, learning how to focus it, learning to feel movements.

In the last third you are applying the techniques. It is the application of energy, with speed but not too fast and still precise. The forms must be developed and practised. The techniques are there to be developed singularly, to be used any time, anywhere. Position of hands is very important here; you must always hold your position. There are three basic hand movements: tan, bong, fook. When you perform fook sau it must be slowly. In case of bong sau the elbow must be higher than the shoulder.

The precise angle of each movement depends on the height of the enemy. If the opponent is the same height you must adjust the position. In practice you must also make it in proportion to the rest of your body. You must make it flat in the case of bong sau, with the shoulder at 90 degrees and then you lower the forearm. Adjust the position to make it higher. If your opponent is taller you must raise the arm. The techniques depend on the height of opponents.

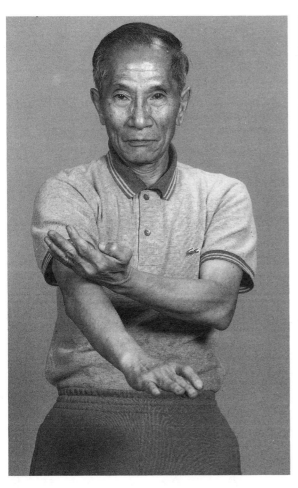

Gan sau

Further Notes

Since it is easy for a beginner to move his shoulder when he should be holding his position, it is most important for him to train in front of the mirror so he can see the middle line clearly. The other reason for having a mirror is to see whether the hands are in place. You need to focus; if there is no mirror you will look down and miss the principle. You need to see your hands without moving your shoulder. Keep a distance between you and the mirror so you can judge whether the actions are properly performed.

So from the moment a student is taught he must find the angles and the precise points?
In Siu Lim Tao you must relax the whole body, don't stiffen, especially in the first part – because if you stiffen the hands you lose inner strength. Make it slow, relax and keep the elbows in. Your hands can indicate whether you are stiff; your hands are soft if you are relaxed. An expert in Siu Lim Tao is one who can keep the elbows in without stiffening, the muscle is still soft; elbows in, hands relaxed. This is very important for a student to master.

For example look at me, my Tan Sau is now in proper position, I don't move my shoulder and my nose and fingertips are in line and precise but if I move my shoulder back I miss the line.

CHUM KIU
(THE SECOND FORM)

This is known as the seeking arm form, or the seeking hand, building the bridge. It is only in the second form that you learn how to reach out to find your opponent; you also learn stepping techniques and three different kicks. You learn how to turn, and how to perform various blocks: tok sau, jut sau, lan sau bong sau. Certain important techniques involved are designed to beat the weaknesses that are inherent in bong sau.

The important points are the correct use of the turning stance in conjunction with the use of bong sau and lan sau to defend against control of the bong sau. In the first section the turning stance is employed with lan sau following on to tok sau/jut sau, then palm strikes. The turning lan sau movement trains for correct power and positioning of the stance with the correct elbow energies trained in the lan sau. In the second section we have the first kick, the front lifting kick,

Chum Kiu (pronounced chum queue) translates as searching or seeking the bridge, i.e. a bridging contact between two people.

Section 1
Trains the horse (stance), the waist and the upper body to coordinate them.

Right: Juen ma – turning stance with double lan sau: to train the stance and waist

followed by the stepping footwork and the rolling arm action to form the bong sau and wu sau movements, which are followed by turning to cover the side with jum sau, turning to face front covering wu sau and striking along the centre line with tan biu sau.

The third section begins with the second kick, the front stamping kick, followed by the stepping footwork with low double bong sau, followed by double biu sau, double jut sau and double palm strikes. Each of these sections is practised to both sides, i.e. with both left and right leads. A left 135° side thrust kick is then followed by turning gum sau techniques, finished off with basic front punches. The emphasis in Chum Kiu is to get the correct positions for the turning stance and to work that in conjunction with the hand techniques such as bong sau to lan sau, turning lan sau, stepping bong sau, palm strikes, etc. The Chum Kiu form deals with using both arms and both legs together, which is a difficult procedure requiring much practice.

Double biu sau – thrusting arm. To cover and receive

Tok sau/jut sau

Section 2
Biu ma with bong sau. Cover – stepping across to receive
and cover

Once contact established turn to deflect with jum sau

Turn to front to recover the jic seen (centre line) with jum sau

Further Notes

Siu Lim Tao is a single-handed movement; even in the second part you are using both hands symmetrically so it is still single-handed. But when you arrive at Chum Kiu you are using both hands for different actions. Moreover, in Siu Lim Tao you don't have to change your stance, but for Chum Kiu you have to change the stance to face different directions. The direction change is important for attack and defence. Finally, in Siu Lim Tao you never move position, you stand on the same spot; but for Chum Kiu you have to change your stance.

Does Chum Kiu have different sections in the way Siu Lim Tao has?
Like Siu Lim Tao, Chum Kiu has three parts, but whereas each Siu Lim Tao part has a distinct purpose, the Chum Kiu parts do not. Chum Kiu's most important part is the one concerned with directional change and defence. The nucleus of Chum Kiu is based on the technique and stance combined together. When you strike a punch, by changing your direction, you already escape the direct counter-punch, but when you put bong sau together with the wu sau you will be safeguarding yourself even more. In bong sau you should not be exerting any pressure, rather you should feel the thrust of the blow by judging; if the blow received is exerting more pressure then you can immediately attack.

So does bong sau technique have a bamboo principle?
More or less. You feel where the pressure comes from, whether from the side, for example. If the blow suddenly retreats because of the bong sau then the bong sau can immediately change into a thrusting action. So, although bong sau is basically a defensive move, it is paving the way for the next attack. But bong sau has a weakness: to use it you have to change your stance and turn your body sideways; you cannot stand as firmly as you could in a full-frontal position. But

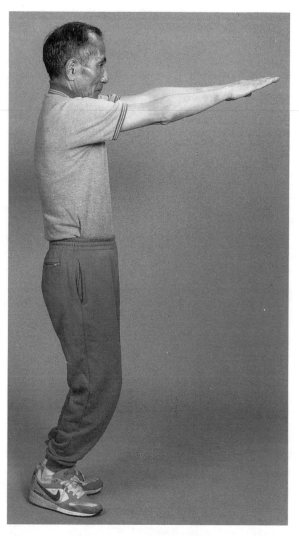

Section 3
Biu ma and double low bong sau – to deflect and cover

Step together with double biu tze sau (thrusting finger strike) to the eyes

despite this weakness, it is still necessary to use bong sau. You must be aware of the weakness of the technique because when you turn your balance is not as firm. If your opponent is stronger than you and you turn sideways to use bong sau he can easily turn you over. So if an opponent pushes you, you have to use a technique to counteract the weakness of this posi-

tion. This movement is the nucleus of the Chum Kiu, the basic element. These last few movements are to defend against thrusts. Using the arm to deflect, you can then move quickly to another movement. The second and third point to notice is how to advance, using sliding steps. You practise all these movements with sliding steps. The third part is how to use a movement

Turn and cover gum sau (pinning hand) – to cover, deflect or where applicable pin

Turn to face front and recover the jic seen (centre line) with a straight punch (yat chi kuen)

when someone presses your hands; you have to thrust, as in double bong sau.

Is the purpose of the movement with the foot to make the body move as one unit in coordination?
Yes. The skill is in coordinating both hands and legs. You have to be powerful in order to be forceful in your attack – just as in any other sport, like soccer. So it is basically one unit.

I know that if a student studies here in the West he asks about progression: for example, how long do you train in Siu Lim Tao, how long in Chum Kiu? Can you give us any idea of the time?
You have to have basic knowledge of Siu Lim Tao and Chum Kiu before you can utilise Biu

Tze; you cannot skip the other two. In the olden days there was a saying that Biu Tze never went out over the doorstep, meaning it was a 'closed door technique'. This is not a literal meaning. It means that only if you have achieved a certain standard of Siu Lim Tao and Chum Kiu can you then be taught the last part, which is Biu Tze. And if anyone has not learnt Biu Tze he cannot claim to be a fully qualified disciple of Wing Chun.

I think it is common now for many Wing Chun teachers to teach Biu Tze before they teach the dummy and the knives. Why is the master different?
When my father Grandmaster Yip Man taught Wing Chun he seldom taught Biu Tze. I agree with my father. If you do not know the basic techniques you will never develop your skill progressively.

Rooftop training in Hong Kong with a visiting group of students

BIU TZE
(THE THIRD FORM)

This third series of movement is known as 'flying fingers' and also as the desperation form when you may need to recover from overextension. It is the development of attacking techniques, moving on to fingers and elbows, more sophisticated concepts of fighting. What you are dealing with is the development of special energy. Initially you must develop the fingertips and hand, and also elbow techniques, also Biu Tze, thrust from underneath to cover any control available, not over, this comes later when you learn how to use elbow and defend against the elbow. Using kup jarn then bui, this is when you go high, a high strike is if you grab on to the

Biu Tze (pronounced byou chee) translates as thrusting fingers form. Also known as Gow Gup Sau – first aid hand. To refine energies and strikes and to recover from missed or over-committed techniques. If it goes wrong, recover using biu tze.

Section 1
Contains 12 elbow strikes
Six kup jarn – downward vertical elbow strike
Two gwoy jarn – horizontal elbow strikes
Four Chair Pie – diagonal elbow strikes

Right: Chair pie – diagonal elbow strike and biu poised beneath

elbow of your opponent, you get him in the head. The next one is lower, palm strike, pull as you lap down, you come on the wrist and you hit low. You cannot reach the head. Double gang sau is a good covering technique, both high and low. Mun sau, then wu sau, fook sau. If you push out you bring it back in to the centre line. Mun sau is a more sophisticated technique. Biu sau is an attack underneath so that the hands are hidden, you grab, lock, give a low hook punch, then relax.

You will find the energy in this development of Biu Tze, focusing it in the fingertips and hands. You should practise hundreds of times. Notice the position; the wrist stays still. The movements of the hand are difficult to develop but the more difficult it is the more energy you will have once you have mastered it.

Close up view, side view: kup, biu, biu, close – notice how the hand comes from the ear, the elbow is high and down.

Biu tze (thrusting fingers) up the jic seen (centre line)

As biu tze strike is pulled back as lap sau, YC executes a low cheng (spade) hand strike to the floating rib

Side view: Traditional opening, finding centre line, energy building exercise of Biu Tze, notice huen sau, it develops the wrist circling movement done with tension, again three kup jarn, focusing on a precise punch, three to the left, three to the right.

The second section – single kup jarn and to the left.

Notice the height of the elbow, it has to go up to drop down. Drop down of target, kup don, if you catch on to the opponent's wrist, hit down low. If you find that double kup you can use it to enter a technique or to defend, if you contact high then you hit low, if you contact with low hand then strike high. Mun sau, again running to fook sau, jun sau exercise. Mun sau, asking hand, fook sau, dan sau, push out, Biu Tze, double grab, lock, from there finishing off exercise.

Section 2
Biu tze sau – thrusting fingers

Double gang sau: jum sau/gan sau

Section 3

Above: Mun sau/wu sau – asking hand with guard hand

Above right: Recover the centre line with jum sau

Right: If forced out from centre line (gil sau) turn to absorb outward force

Double grab in front

Turn with double lap sau (deflecting hand)

Turn sharply to face front with an upward front punch arching in and up the centre line

Further Notes

Biu Tze basically consists of attacking techniques. Another explanation of Biu Tze is that it is for attacking the eyes. It is not easy for you to attack your opponent's eyes if he responds quickly. In this case Biu Tze can be used continuously with other forms to attack or defend. If you fail to attack with Biu Tze, if both hands are in contact, you can still make contact with the elbows. Then if he punches you or receives a punch from you, you have feeling with the hands. The worst thing during Chi Sau practice is if you miss one or both hands of the opponent. It is dangerous for you to miss the hands because the hand you miss is the one that hits you. So, in Wing Chun, Chi Sau is very important, the constant contact of the hands. If you miss one or both hands then that is what mun sau is for – to reach out and get it. In terms of feeling you can never resist if master uses man sau (direct translation – to ask for your hands). If you don't reach out your hands you will be hit. Mun sau can be used for your first strike; it is used to achieve the first punch, the first contact, to bridge the distance. It is part of the defending form involved in Biu Tze. Remember this is usually used for single hand contact, which is common in Biu Tze. So if you are good at mun sau you should be good at making contact. Mun sau is facing, and reaching out hands continuously; these movements are not supposed to be Biu Tze but are involved. If you punch, this is lap sau. If your opponent punches you and draws back power correctly, you can never use lap sau, but if he punches and he uses his hands you can still use lap sau. Remember three points:

- Grip around the wrist, control the elbow. If you do not block his elbow he will attack you with it.
- When you resist the hands don't push; you should pull hard downwards so that your opponent will bend forward.

Biu Tze applications

Double lap sau (deflecting hands)

Above: The opponent's punch is deflected by YC who turns with double lap sau (notice the wrist and elbow control)

YC follows with a front kick . . .

. . . which strikes to the hip joint destroying his opponent's balance

YC uses the momentum (kinetic energy) gained by putting his foot to the floor to feed a punch to the ribs (whilst covering his opponent's elbow with his left hand).

YC deflects his opponent's strike with a turn and double lap sau

Using his left hand to control his opponent's arm at the elbow, YC starts to move in and close the distance . . .

 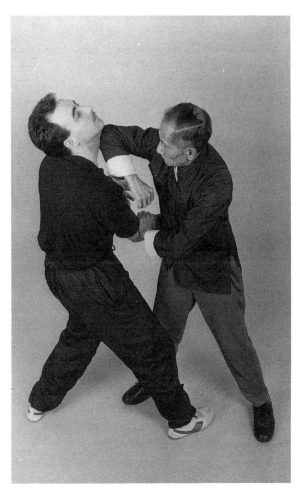

. . . rolling kup jarn (vertical elbow) over the strike . . .

and driving the vertical elbow strike down into his opponent's neck, whilst controlling his opponent's lead leg with his knee.

• When you seize the hand never hold it too tight because when you push you will fall down. If you do lap sau that way your opponent will use his elbow to attack you. Don't keep the hold too strong because you will miss one hand. Once you achieve the movement, let go.

YC receives the strike by turning to avoid and deflecting with double lap sau

These are the main movements of Biu Tze. There is a saying in the Buddhist scripture that if you practise Biu Tze you can see the moon; but you can never reach the moon by doing Biu Tze.

Is this to give some guidance to the student, this point about reaching the moon?
If you ask me where the moon is, I will point to it for you; if you are clever you will follow my finger, a foolish man will take my finger as the moon. In other words, the moon is equal to the truth, so if you ask for the truth I will show you; but the finger is not the truth. So, in the case of each form, just like the finger it can be used for attack and defence at the same time. Bong sau is not just for blocking a punch, it can be also used for attack.

Let me explain. There are twelve downward (not horizontal) strikes using the elbows in Biu Tze – twelve kup jarn. In many martial arts the strikes are horizontal, but in Biu Tze they are downward; they are for close distance attack, if the opponent is so close that you cannot punch; sometimes you can only use the elbows to strike. If you can perform them properly these blows are strong enough.

But if you continually bang your elbow against a bag can you cause damage to yourself?
Not if it is just an empty strike.

Can you damage your body or neck through practice?
Never practise elbow strikes with a sand bag, never, because the shock of striking the elbow against a solid object can cause damage to the spine.

Double lap sau controls

YC cuts back to the centre line with a low rising punch to the floating rib.

YC recovers from an over-committed bong sau by thrusting biu tze up the centre line from beneath the bong sau

. . . and thrusting towards his opponent's eyes to dissuade him from stepping further forward

Why not?

Because it can cause serious damage to the spine. When you punch, you have the elbow to absorb the impact and, moreover, it is not easy for you to use all your strength. But in the case of an elbow strike you use the power of your whole body. Even a beginner can suffer damage using this strike because the body is soft, and the impact is not absorbed as it is for a punch.

QUESTIONS AND ANSWERS:
YIP CHUN IN DIALOGUE
WITH HIS STUDENTS

Many teachers talk about secrets but you seem to teach as much as the students can learn. Many teachers hold back; how do you feel about this?

I say Wing Chun should not be taught like that. For example, it is possible to introduce everything within one year: Siu Lim Tao, Chum Kiu, Biu Tze, wooden dummy, Baat Cham Dao (butterfly knives), Wing Chun Long Pole and Chi Sau, and let the students improve and improve. It is like a safe full of money; you need the key, but you only get the key through Chi Sau – even then you still have a long way to go. You may have the theory but you need training and to practise with each other. Learning forms is not the final thing, you must practise. In Wing Chun it is most important how to feel each movement, each form and make it more fluent and create a smooth flow of actions. As for masters who do not teach all the techniques to the students, it might be because they have little else to teach and will hold things back. Many of them have only been training for a short time and then they turn themselves into masters. If a master is advanced in Wing Chun he will not conceal anything. The development of skill is unlimited.

How do you see the effect of training on students? What changes take place? Are the students more con-fident – does Wing Chun affect them psychologically?

The answer to that must come from the students themselves. But many have told me that they have grown in confidence because they now know they can defend and attack at will.

After students have been taught, and after they have practised Chi Sau, what is it that stops them from reaching a higher level? At what point do they stop developing?

They do not use force correctly! In other forms of Kung Fu or in Karate and other martial arts, you tend to use force all the time and it limits your development of control. In Wing Chun knowing the right moment to use force is critical. The most difficult thing is releasing pressure immediately after you have exerted it. It is easy to forget and this bars you from moving on and advancing to another stage.

Do you think that this is because our society is influenced by force, size and power, and psychologically we cannot accept that skill can defeat brute force?

I think it is not to do with society, it is just that it is hard for people to put together the two contrasting concepts, the two different movements of using force and relaxing at the same time. This technique takes a long time to fully master.

I feel that whether Wing Chun changes one's character has a lot to do with the teacher's everyday behaviour, his personality. Usually, to practise all forms of Wing Chun takes at least three years and during this time you learn a lot about the master's personality; it has nothing to do with Wing Chun itself. This problem is not limited to Wing Chun, but is common to all forms of Kung Fu, because of the teaching process. If a master induces you to fight with people to test you, this is a form of brainwashing, it is dangerous. The master wants to point out the difference between the way he would settle a dispute between disciples and the way an exponent of another form of Kung Fu would settle it.

In many forms of Kung Fu the relationship between the master and the students has a barrier in between. Some masters instruct the students to wear a form of uniform, some even make them perform rituals; they try to be supreme. What Grandmaster Yip Man did was to treat students as equals, and after training he and his students were friends. Some people think there should be a barrier. Even Grandmaster Yip Man was criticised for being too friendly.

I say there should be no barriers, the information should flow. Wing Chun teachers should be friends with their students, there is no ceremony. We are not looking for slaves. A student will respect a master if he can learn what he wants, not simply because the master demands respect.

Do you think today's students study as hard as in the past?
Nowadays they are lazy, they think our form is too soft; they want Karate and kicks, they want to make it like Lee Jun Fan (Bruce Lee).

In Fatschan do many people still study Wing Chun?
Last year they had a class of students but I don't know about this year.

How far back does Wing Chun go in Fatshan? How many generations before you started practising?
It is a very long time ago and it is difficult to know how many generations practised. By the end of the Sung dynasty there was a very famous scholar, Wong Yung Min. He was an expert and well educated in Confucius. He gave a positive push to Confucius and he was a famous successor. One of the theories put forward was 'in order to achieve something there are two things involved: theory and practice'.

Theory is the knowledge and practice means action – it does not mean mixing the two points together. Knowledge is a concept, just like the punching principles of Wing Chun, and practice is the action, after you have mastered the theories. But you must put the theory into practice otherwise it is useless. You must make use of what you have learned. This does not mean that you have to practise immediately after you have obtained the knowledge, but once you have learned something and have the knowledge, you must test it yourself. During practice you can find out whether there is a much better theory. There must be more theories obtained during training. It is the accumulation of knowledge, like a snowball; there is knowledge, then action, then knowledge, then action and so on until you become better and improve your future. Without practice, knowledge is useless; after practice you must seek more knowledge to develop the art.

How does Wing Chun relate to nature?
Wing Chun people should respect nature. For example, in your stance the distance between the insides of the heels depends on your height. If you twist and bend forward this is wrong; the body should be in balance as in nature, according to your height, not because of doctrines or principles. The gap between the insides of the heels should be the width of the shoulders.

This is linked to a more far-reaching principle. One of the main theories of Confucius is Chung Yung. Chung means the middle line or centre line, Yung means harmony. The meaning of harmony is not to overdo it, to be moderate. The Chinese were greatly influenced by these theories.

For example, take a manager of a company. He should have principles in order to manage everything; this can be explained as Chung. If this manager does everything by sticking to the principles and rules, he cannot be sacked: he may be successful, but he is going to create ill-feeling within the company and things will become a mess. He should be flexible and this will create harmony (Yung). Therefore everything should be based on the rules but still be flexible, although not straying too far from the principles. You have to learn to master the point between principles and flexibility. If you can hold this point, this is what you can get from this book, Chung Yung.

In order to master the way of the centre line, the moderate way of handling things, you must train a lot. The theories of Chung Yung are like Chi Sau in Wing Chun. When my students first study Siu Lim Tao I will say, pay a lot of attention to the centre line. I will ask them to train with a mirror. In the case of real fighting the centre line means precision; you must get a strong hold on the centre line first. The centre line is a must but it is not enough. When fighting, whether attacking or defending, to stick strictly to the centre line without changing it is wrong. Sometimes you must move to the left or right a little bit. You must also make constant adjustments.

How do you apply this principle?
In Chung Yung theory only experience will tell and you can only obtain this through Chi Sau. That is why you must keep the centre line during Chi Sau. As to how much you can move, again only the experience you achieve through Chi Sau will tell you. Another Chung Yung tenet is, do something in order to achieve and then stop; that is enough, never push too far. Go to the point but do not overreach.

Is overreaching just as dangerous as losing the centre line?
Yes. Too much is worse than not enough. If there is too much attention to the centre line then that is wrong; going too far is worse. The first point is to understand the middle line, the second point is the point of releasing energy, don't make it too much, that is what Yung means. In terms of Wing Chun we pay a lot of attention to this. This shows two aspects of Chi Sau – how to use power correctly and too much pressure is a waste of energy.

Is the centre line horizontal or vertical?
It should be vertical! In order to keep a proper stance we must adjust it depending on the situation, because if you keep a rigid stance it is not good enough, you will get tired. You can change your stance without losing the centre line. Remember Bruce Lee – he jumped around all the time but it does not mean he lost the centre line. In Bruce Lee's mind there was a stance but it was flexible. When he made a strike he always seemed to make a strike from a balanced position despite the dramatic movements. When he jumped there was no stance but when he punched there was a good stance.

In all kinds of Wing Chun techniques, pak sau and lap sau, for example, if the master punches off line the elbow of the opponent will block the punch so the master must use pak sau. The purpose of pak sau is to get the punch in line.

In the case of lap sau as long as he can punch, it is enough. Once you achieve this it is enough, there is no need to grab the hands after punching; if the opponent pushes you, you will fall down. These fighting techniques come from the theory of Chung Yung.

When you practise with your students you do not seem to move quickly to respond, but whenever a technique is required it is there. This is difficult for me to understand, this level of skill – moving just enough. Can you explain how you apply these principles?

To be fast is not the point. I have done Chi Sau lots of times and I will punch at different speeds depending on the situation. So being fast is not the point; how to make it is the point. Speed depends on the conditions. If two opponents are fast, the fastest one will win, but they will continue to see how to attack again, so in Chi Sau, as in real fighting, there should be rhythm.

So you are able to respond so quickly because you can read the energy of the other person? Is this a particular skill?
Yes, I can sense the power of the opponent and you can only achieve this through feeling.

Which element in the Wing Chun system do you feel that all the techniques developed from: is it Chi Sau or is the starting point the wooden dummy?
This is very important; it is about techniques. The purpose of practising with a wooden man is for training in techniques. The wooden dummy is like a dead man, just for basic training in Siu Lim Tao, Chum Kiu and Biu Tze. But for Chi Sau you have a real man, a real opponent to practise with. The point of training with a wooden man is that its distance from you is fixed, which helps you learn the correct fighting distance between you and your enemy. But when you fight with a real opponent your reactions are trained; practising with a real opponent is the best way to improve.

I was told that the dummy is to practise the Ging (energy) for the techniques?
No – training with the dummy does not mean training with inner strength. There are three things that can never be trained with the wooden dummy: feeling, reactions and the basic techniques of real contact with an opponent. A live man can counter-attack. Both the dummy and real opponents are for training your ability, and both have different purposes. This is my personal opinion. At the very beginning you should train with the dummy and then go to Chi Sau.

Is there Taoist or Buddhist influence within Wing Chun?
There is one thing we are sure of: the development of Wing Chun is in some way related to Chinese culture and philosophy. It could also have been influenced to some extent by Buddhist or Taoist philosophy. But I feel Wing Chun is very practical and do not want to make it too metaphysical or abstract.

When I watch you, you do not seem to stick too much to any one technique and your strongest point appears to be that you are immediately ready to make a change quicker than anybody because you are not over-attached to a successful movement. Can you explain?
During Wing Chun training there are a number of possibilities you can be subjected to, in case you are attacked, and you must bear in mind what kind of reaction your opponent will make.

When you defend, you must defend by reaction, but when you do a certain kind of movement by reaction, you must bear in mind what your opponent will do next time. That reaction is objective; you have to think of the other steps – your opponent's reaction.

Are you saying that you are able to estimate what your opponent's next techniques are likely to be?
Yes, just like when playing chess, anticipation is very important in the whole system of Chi Sau. You might say there is no difference in the early stages but sooner or later there are changes. You must think before you react. If you know nothing about chess there is no way you can match an expert; he will control everything. Chi Sau is like playing chess.

Right: wooden dummy practice

In Siu Lim Tao are the movements exactly the same as we use in Chi Sau?

Siu Lim Tao has many technical aspects. To explain how it works, take the example of tan sau. It brings forth long series of changes; there is no fixed rule or way to explain how tan sau works. Tan sau is used to block the first punch; this means that it is for defence – but at the same time this blocking could be a way of attack. Bong sau can also be used in attack and not just for defence.

So bong sau is not just used to block, as some people believe; it also has other elements?

Yes. There are three main movements of the hands, these are the three main forms, and they allow defence to be changed into attack.

Why is it that, although students try to do what you say, they cannot come near to your level of technique, which seems beyond everyone? What stops others from reaching that level?

The problem with most students is that they are just paying attention to one technique and its use in either attack or defence; they only remember one way of action. It is important to pay attention to the whole system of Chi Sau. When fighting with the dummy there is no reaction so you cannot practise how to deal with an opponent's reaction – you cannot imagine it, for example. In Wing Chun it is very important for you to practise and at the same time bear in mind that your enemy is alive, not dead; he can always react. There are thousands of ways to react. So it is very important for you to study the whole system of Chi Sau, not just one or two movements.

Otherwise you become inflexible and cannot adjust?

This is what I am emphasising. When punching,

Left: wooden dummy practice

you must bear in mind your opponent is alive, he can react and punch back and how you react to that is crucially important.

What is the recommended training schedule for someone who wants to practise Chi Sau and Siu Lim Tao. How do you feel they should introduce Siu Lim Tao within personal practice, time frequency, etc.?

Historically it was stated that Siu Lim Tao should be practised for three years before progression. Siu Lim Tao is the first form of Wing Chun, the basic form. You can polish your fundamental techniques through Siu Lim Tao. There are three main parts in Siu Lim Tao. Inner strength is one (this does not mean power). For example, if you knocked me with your elbow, and I want to hit you, if you have the inner strength I cannot achieve it this way. You can try. Inner strength is not power. It is fixed so you cannot move it. That is why we have to practise Siu Lim Tao in order to train the inner strength and keep the correct position to block punches.

In Western boxing they stress that you should keep your elbows in, so is there some parallel?

There might be a similar principle. Both boxing and Chinese Kung Fu have a history. During Chi Sau I advise you to keep your elbows in.

One famous boxer (Jack Dempsey) said the energy runs underneath the bottom of the arm; is this similar?

Yes, that is correct. This theory is similar to Wing Chun. The second part of Siu Lim Tao is for training in the proper use of power and inner strength.

I recommend that students begin to practise Chi Sau after they have learnt Siu Lim Tao. This is because it keeps them interested. If students only practise the form they will lose interest, but if Chi Sau practice comes next the student will understand why he has been doing the exercises. I prefer to finish teaching Siu Lim Tao first. In order to make proper progress, when you practise the first part of Siu Lim Tao it must be slow, as slow as possible, concentrating on keeping the elbow in and developing inner strength.

If the individual wants to take a long time is that OK?
Yes, the longer the better. Bear in mind that it is not right to say: 'OK, I have done this thousands of times, I am an expert.' The most important thing is your attitude. Are you slow enough in action? Do you keep your elbows in at all times? The one who can practise Siu Lim Tao as slowly as possible will achieve more and have inner strength. Take it easy, don't rush.

In the West, people want to learn and move on too quickly to the next step – do you agree?
Yes. If someone is very bad at Siu Lim Tao and tries to learn it too fast his inner strength will not be good, so he will have to depend on skills, but he may not have good skills. You have to become objective. Someone who develops inner strength can be objective.

Of course, you can use the techniques and make it up with skills but you must become objective, and even as you get better you must remain objective. So skill or techniques and inner strength are two different things. You have to master them both.

During the second and third parts each movement is properly performed. In tan sau practice you can be slow, but in real fighting you cannot use tan sau that slow. And keep a proper stance. For a beginner there is naturally movement of the shoulders, but only the hands should move, not the shoulders.

So wobbling means losing energy?
No, it is because of wrong positioning.

Can you tell us about Grandmaster Yip Man and his training?
Grandmaster Yip Man started Kung Fu training in Fatshan province at the age of seven and continued until he was thirteen. His master, Chan Wah Soon, passed away when Yip Man was thir-

teen, and just before he died he told one of his seniors, Ng Chung So, to be responsible for taking care of Yip Man in order to make him a great master. Yip Man followed Ng Chung So for two years to further his studies in Wing Chun. At the age of fifteen Yip Man and a fellow classmate, Un Ki Sen, went to Hong Kong to study at St Stephen's College, and there by coincidence Yip Man met Leung Bik, the son of Leung Jan. Yip Man studied Wing Chun under Master Leung Bik for three years. This is roughly the history of his training, and according to Grandmaster Yip Man what he really learned about Wing Chun was obtained during his time in Hong Kong. There are two reasons for this:

1) Grandmaster Yip Man says there is some theory that seems to be untouchable in Wing Chun and when he was in his boyhood he was not able to catch the idea.

2) His first master, Master Chan Wah Soon, was not quite an educated person, and it is better for one to be well educated in order to study the arts and get more understanding from them. As for the theory of Wing Chun, Master Chan Wah Soon did not know much about it, so frankly Grandmaster Yip Man did not receive much knowledge about the arts from him. When he studied Wing Chun with Leung Bik, Yip Man was much older and Leung Bik was quite experienced and with better understanding of Wing Chun.

So Grandmaster Yip Man received the real knowledge of Wing Chun when he was an adult.

What about his way of teaching Wing Chun?
He was quite a traditional person because he studied a lot of books about Chinese history and culture. He was rather conservative in his personality. He did not intend to teach Kung Fu because he said that teaching Kung Fu meant teaching people how to fight and it would be

unlucky according to Buddhist theory (the cause and the results). So even though Grandmaster Yip Man was skilful in Wing Chun Kung Fu and many people asked him to teach it, he still rejected them. But, in fact, over two periods Grandmaster Yip Man suffered quite a lot and was therefore forced to teach Kung Fu.

The first period was the time when the Japanese raided China in the Second World War. At that time he was teaching several students in Fatshan in China (there are one or two students who still teach Wing Chun in Fatshan).

During the second period he worked for the National Government of Chang Kai Shek as quite a high-ranking officer. After the Communists took over he was forced to go to Hong Kong in order to make a living and he had to teach Kung Fu in Hong Kong. Grandmaster Yip Man could not imagine that his teaching would influence the coming developments of Wing Chun in the whole world. Another way in which he was conservative was in his refusal to teach Wing Chun to foreigners; so if there are any Westerners who claim that they were his students, they are lying. Grandmaster Yip Man said Wing Chun was a treasure of China and should be held in respect.

Did he ever teach women?
Yes, at the very beginning he taught some lady students, but not so many. More men practise Kung Fu than women.

So did he teach in the same way as you teach now; for example teaching the techniques quickly and then practising Chi Sau with the students?
This is a very important point. I appreciate more about the teaching of Kung Fu than the knowledge of his Wing Chun. Just before teaching, Grandmaster Yip Man tended to have a talk with each student to try to understand his education, his work, study timetable, personality, etc., before he started teaching him. He took a special note of the size of the student's body, his height,

etc. So all the students of Grandmaster Yip Man achieved a lot. Yip Man also tended to improve his way of teaching gradually, and in this way he was not especially conservative.

So he developed it from the original way to make it more scientific?
Yes, for example, Siu Lim Tao or wooden dummy techniques. His first students learned from these kind of techniques. The grandmaster was making developments. Yip Man emphasised that we have to learn from experience to improve the art and broaden our knowledge. There should be constant development.

In those days when Grandmaster Yip Man was teaching in Hong Kong, was it difficult to establish himself in order to teach? Were there problems from other schools of Kung Fu?
He started his teaching at the Chinese Restaurant Markets Unions, and encountered no problems. No one sought trouble because he was famous, very famous, in South East China; so when he started teaching many people knew who he was.

How could people know he was famous?
Because since his arrival in Hong Kong at the age of fifteen, he was famous in Kung Fu, fighting with other Kung Fu instructors.

In Chinese culture they talk about the excellences to be achieved; what are these?
Four of the most famous books belong to the Confucius school: *Chung Yung, Great Learning, Man Chi* and *Lung Yu*. There are another six (making ten altogether). *Poetry, Study of Yik, Study of Chinese Politeness, Study of Chinese Philosophy, Study of Music, Study of Chun Chow* (Dynasty of Confucius).

Great Learning asks people to look for knowledge; *Lung Yu* is theoretical, instructing people how to be successful, with attention also given to Chinese morality. *Chung Yung* is typical Chinese philosophy. *Man Chi* was for students of Confucius and evaluated his theories. The book of the Chow is about the Chow dynasty just before the Confucius period. The *Study of Yik* is about Chinese philosophies and the physical part. The book of poetry is about Chinese politeness and moralities.

The appeal of Wing Chun for many people seems to be that it appeals to people to better their education because it does not rely on brute force. In your travels do you find that students of Wing Chun are better educated?

I go to Europe mainly for seminars, and have met a lot of Wing Chun followers. Because of the language barrier I do not know about their educational background. Of course most questions asked by students at seminars are about Chinese Kung Fu and it is possible to tell a little about the students' background from their questions, but what they asked was mainly on the technical side of Wing Chun. Trevor was the most educated person I have met during these trips. That was in Newcastle.

Do you feel other styles of Kung Fu are designed for drama rather than efficiency? Whereas Wing Chun is pure efficiency, there are no techniques to make it more appealing. If we consider Wing Chun is part of a general group, when many other groups have different techniques, is Wing Chun the bridge between the drama and the efficiency?

Wing Chun is not designed for drama. We have to see Kung Fu as it evolved in a primitive age, when we had to fight to live, to fight the beast as well as humans. Since then Kung Fu has developed in two parallel lines. One way is for drama purposes, accompanied by music, for dancing as well as stage performance, accompanied by the clapping of hands; the second way is for efficiency, the main purpose being to defend and fight. If you want to achieve efficiency you don't concern yourself with looking good; the purpose is to beat your opponent in

the fastest way, so it will not be pretty. It is not meant to be observed by an audience. Very often Kung Fu used for dramatic purposes is not efficient. Both ways of Kung Fu have followers so two ways have developed over the years. Frankly speaking, Wing Chun is not for drama, it is for efficiency. Those who perform Kung Fu for drama deny that it is not efficient, but even if you walk every morning you will get a healthy body. Sometimes students of other styles of Kung Fu make the excuse for getting a healthy body the fact that at first they are taught that they will be unable to achieve the defence skills unless they are fit. When you are practising Chi Sau as well as other styles, forget everything and let your brain rest in a calm position. Then you will be able to succeed. Students who have practised Wing Chun for a long time should not need to be reminded that they shouldn't fight with people, because they are aware that they have the ability and so they should control their tempers and try not to have disputes with others; that is the moral of Kung Fu that people should adhere to.

So they should realise the responsibility they have because they possess the techniques?

Those who have only learned Kung Fu for say a few months may try to fight with others; but the longer they learn the better will be their temper. As regards those who have learned Wing Chun for a long time, they all have healthy bodies, yet at the same time have acquired practical self-defence skills.

Does Wing Chun attract more mature people, as compared to other branches of Kung Fu, Karate, etc.?

Old people can do it! I first practised Siu Lim Tao at about seven years of age, Wing Chun at thirty-seven. My oldest student is fifty-one.

Is there confusion about modified and traditional forms?

I have never heard of so-called modified Wing

Chun. But Wing Chun is becoming popular internationally, and many people teach false forms of real Wing Chun; there are so many brands, like perfumes or fashion houses. There are many branches with many different names because it is so popular. Beware of imitations.

So if a Western student wants to learn Wing Chun and he does not know how to judge a good teacher, what advice could the master give him?

This is quite a problem, but there is one way to test if your teacher is a real master of Wing Chun. If the master is willing to be attacked by you during Chi Sau he is a real Wing Chun master. If he punches back then he is not a good Wing Chun master because he is afraid of being punched by you again. You only attack in terms of defence. If the master is going to be attacked and only makes a little touch, mock fighting, he is good; if he punches back heavily then he is not a good master. In fact a good master will instruct you to attack, knowing you do not have a chance, you cannot hit him because he is a master. Nobody, including the master, is willing to be hit by students. If the master is not strong enough to receive your attack he will not ask you to attack and will just do defence. In this case he will punch you first to make you afraid so you will not punch him back. This is how you can tell which one is the good master.

How was a young boy such as Bruce Lee able to study with Grandmaster Yip Man?

He was a form four student when he started, just like a son. Fourteen is a good age to start learning Wing Chun.

What about the Jeet Kune Do of Bruce Lee?

Bruce Lee was a born fighter as well as a film star. He understood both these things. He understood that it was not good for him to perform Wing Chun fight styles in movies as they were not good fighting styles for a movie. So in order to make a good Kung Fu movie he had to fight with a beautiful style, which is against the principals of Wing Chun. If he had performed Wing Chun in a movie his seniors would have given him a lot of criticism, so he was clever enough to avoid this by creating the style Jeet Kune Do. 'If I create the style, you cannot criticise it.' Before Bruce Lee changed the name of his Kung Fu to Jeet Kune Do he asked for the agreement of Grandmaster Yip Man and I was present. He asked his permission to change the name of his Kung Fu to Jeet Kune Do as it was making money. He was a clever guy and was respectful enough to ask Grandmaster Yip Man to make these changes because he was to make a movie and didn't want to cause problems for the Wing Chun families.

In the future maybe more and more people will want to visit Hong Kong and study with you. If people can afford to travel, may they first write to ask if they can be accepted?

Yes, write to me. People are becoming passionate about Wing Chun. You may also study when I am in London for seminars.

But once people read this question-and-answer series they will tend to ask the question, 'How long will it take for me to finish the course?'

That depends on your attitude to study. Are you hard-working? Are you serious? What about your ability to study? There are many factors.

How quickly is it possible to learn?

Well, actually Siu Lim Tao, wooden dummy techniques and Baat Cham Dao and the Long Staff I can teach quite easily in one or two months and you can make it. Chi Sau takes unlimited study; in this discipline I am still not satisfied with my own performance – it's like that for all students.

When can someone expect to finish their study?

I can teach the techniques within a short period of time but the development of Chi Sau, for example, is unlimited, and there can be no guarantees. If you are lazy how can you make it? For Siu Lim Tao and wooden dummy there are fixed forms which can be taught according to a schedule. You can learn the three forms in one month, and it will take another month for knives and wooden dummy techniques. Before doing Baat Cham knives you must first finish your study of Siu Lim Tao, Chum Kiu and Biu Tze. If you already have knowledge of the three forms I can then teach you the Baat Cham Dao techniques. Generally, we expect people to finish the three forms first.

THE DOCTRINE OF THE MEAN

Notes on Confucius

The Chinese have always had a great regard for Confucius, and now he has even been rehabilitated in mainland China after the Cultural Revolution.

Yip Chun, by uniting the principles of Wing Chun with 'Chung Yung' philosophy, brings Wing Chun back to what is perhaps its spiritual home.

Two thousand five hundred years ago, a full 500 years before Jesus Christ, Confucius said, 'Do not do unto others that which you would not have them do unto you'. Confucius was a teacher, and in China he is considered the teacher of teachers. Throughout the centuries his thoughts have resonated and ring true even today, even though he has been trivialised in the English language thanks to phrases beginning, 'Confucius say . . .'.

In the Doctrine of the Mean, Confucius talks of holding on to principles, yet not to the exclusion of the human condition. And in practical terms there is little use in holding on to principles regardless of reality. The principles he lays down are for those who teach and the relationships they have with the rest of society. Is not philosophy the learning of how to live with your fellow man?

This umbelicus between philosophical thought and the practice of Chi Sau, or 'sticking hands', will carry Wing Chun into the future.

The Text

My master, the philosopher Ch'ang, says: 'Being without inclination to either side is called chung; *admitting of no change is called* yung. *By* chung *is denoted the correct course to be pursued by all under heaven; by* yung *is denoted the fixed principle regulating all under heaven. This work contains the law of the mind, which was handed down from one to another, in the Confucian school, till Tsze-sze, fearing lest in the course of time errors should arise about it, committed it to writing, and delivered it to Mencius. The Book first speaks of one principle; it next spreads this out, and embraces all things; finally, it returns and gathers them all up under the one principle. Unroll it, and it fills the universe; roll it up, and it retires and lies hid in mysteriousness. The relish of it is inexhaustible. The whole of it is solid learning. When the skilful reader has explored it with delight till he has apprehended it, he may carry it into practice all his life, and will find that it cannot be exhausted.'*

Legge, James (translator)

PERSONAL SOURCE OF SOCIAL HARMONY

What Nature provides is called 'one's own nature'. Developing in accordance with one's own nature is called 'the way of self-realisation'. Proper pursuit of the way of self-realisation is called 'maturity'.

One's own nature cannot be disowned. If it could be disowned, it would not be one's own nature. Hence, a wise man pays attention to it and is concerned about it, even when it is not apparent and when it does not call attention to itself.

One's external appearance is nothing more than an expression of one's invisible interior, and one's outward manifestation reveals only what is inside. Therefore the wise man is concerned about his own self.

Being unconcerned about attitudes toward others and by others involving feeling pleased, angered, grieved, or joyful is called 'one's genuine personal nature'. Being concerned about such attitudes, each in its appropriate way, is called 'one's genuine social nature'.

This 'genuine personal nature' is the primary source from which all that is social develops. This 'genuine social nature' is the means whereby everyone obtains happiness.

When our 'genuine personal nature' and 'genuine social nature' mutually supplement each other perpetually, then conditions everywhere remain wholesome, and everything thrives and prospers.

DIFFICULTIES IN SELF-DEVELOPMENT

The wise man retains his genuine personal nature. The foolish man does the opposite.

A wise man is wise because he always retains his genuine personal nature, and the foolish man does the opposite because, being foolish, he fails to appreciate what is good.

One's genuine personal nature is self-sufficient. But how few people can maintain it for a long time!

I know why the course of one's genuine personal nature is not pursued. Men of achievement try to surpass it. The inept fail to maintain it.

I know why the course of one's genuine personal nature is not understood. The ambitious overestimate it. The lazy fail to appreciate it.

All men eat and drink. But there are few whose taste tells them when they have had precisely enough.

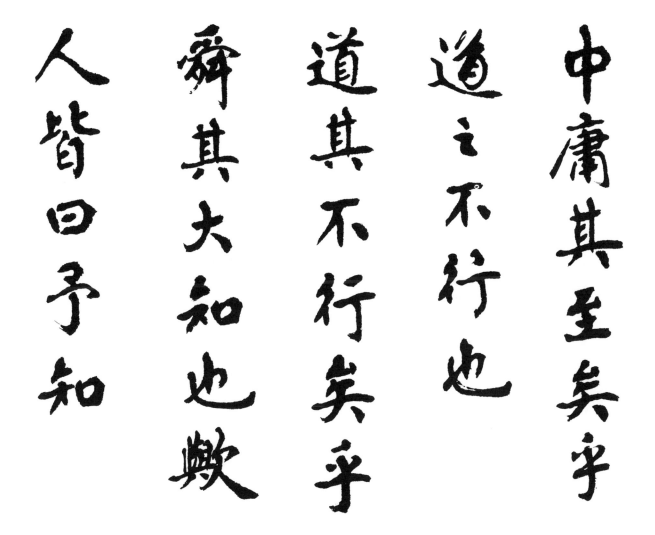

人皆曰予知　舜其大知也歟　道其不行矣乎　道之不行也　中庸其至矣乎

Regrettable indeed is this failure to follow one's genuine personal nature.

Consider the sage, for example, who has great wisdom. He likes to inquire and to examine the views expressed, no matter how simple. He ignores what is bad and elicits what is good. By apprehending opposing extremes, he makes clear the middle way. Such is the sage's disposition.

Everyone thinks, 'I am wise.' But being urged onward, they become ensnared unawares. Everyone believes, 'I am successful.'

But even when they happen to follow their own true nature, they cannot persist in following it for a whole month.

A wise man chooses to follow his genuine nature. When he perfects his behaviour in any way, he sticks to it, appreciates it, and never departs from it.

One may be able to govern one's country, one's state, and one's family perfectly, to forgo honor and prosperity, and to risk death without hesitation, without being able to realise one's own genuine nature.

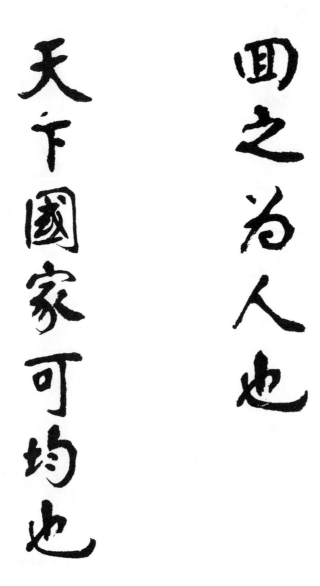

PERSONAL VIRTUE EXEMPLIFIED

Tzu Lu inquired about virtue.

Confucius replied: 'Do you mean "Southern virtue" or "Northern virtue" or the virtue which is best for you?'

Southern people idealise patience and gentleness, readiness to help others, without wanting to punish mistreatment. Southern gentlemen embody these virtues.

Northern people admire readiness to fight and to risk death without hesitation. Northern heroes emulate these virtues.

However, the wise man lives in harmony with others without being led astray by them. How wholesome is his virtue!

He establishes himself in the middle way without leaning towards either side. How intelligent is his virtue!

When propitious practices prevail in public affairs, he remains undeviating in his private life. How reliable is his virtue!

When vicious practices prevail in public affairs, he still retains his virtuous habits without modification even in the face of death. How enduring is his virtue!

PRETENSION IS UNWISE

To investigate the mysterious and to perform the spectacular for the sake of future reputation is something which I will not do.

The wise man emulates Nature in all his ways. To do so in only some ways is not enough.

The wise man accepts his genuine nature. Even though he may be completely unknown, ignored by everyone, he lives without remorse. Only one who is saintly can do this.

NATURE'S WAY IS SUFFICIENT

Nature, which the wise man emulates, is apparent everywhere but also hidden in each thing.

The most ignorant people have some knowledge of it, yet even the wisest of men cannot comprehend it fully. The most degenerate people embody it somewhat, but even the wisest of men cannot emulate it perfectly. For, magnificent as the universe is, man still wants it to be different.

So, when the learned man expresses his ideals of greatness, the actual world does not fully exemplify them. And when he expresses his ideals of minute distinctions, nothing in the actual world can embody them.

It is written in the *Book of Verses*: 'The eagle soars high up in the

sky and the shark dives down into the depths.' This saying illustrates how Nature extends above and below.

The social nature of the wise man originates from the simplest relations between men and women; it grows to full maturity, it comprehends everything in the world.

NATURE'S WAY IS SELF-CORRECTING

Nature's way is not something apart from men. When a man pursues a way which separates him from men, it is not Nature's way.

In the *Book of Verses* it is written: 'When one moulds an axe handle, his pattern is not far away.' The model for the handle is in the hand which grasps it, even though when we compare them, they appear different. So likewise, the wise man influences men by appealing to their natures. When they revert to nature's way, he stops.

When one develops one's nature most fully, one finds that the principles of fidelity and mutuality are not something apart from one's nature. Whatever you do not want done to you, do not do to others.

The nature of a wise man includes four achievements, none of which I have attained:

1) To appreciate my father as I wish my son to appreciate me. This I have not been able to do.
2) To serve my superior officers as I desire my subordinate officials to serve me. This I have not been able to do.
3) To treat my elder brother in the same way I would expect my younger brother to treat me. This I have not been able to do.
4) To be as considerate of friends as I would like to have my friends be considerate of me. This I have not been able to do.

The wise man is attentive to both his behaviour and his speech. Whenever his behaviour becomes deficient, the wise man tries to correct it. Whenever his speech becomes annoying, he restrains himself. Thus, while speaking, he gives constant attention to his actions, and, when acting, he gives constant attention to his speaking. Should not a wise man be thus constantly attentive?

HUMILITY IS WISE

The wise man adapts himself appropriately to each situation. He does not desire to make it different.

When he finds himself amid wealth and dignity, he conducts himself as one who is worthy and esteemed.

When he finds himself among the poor and despised, he behaves in ways appropriate to poverty and disdain.

When he finds himself in a foreign civilisation, he adapts himself to foreign customs.

When he finds himself in distress and affliction, he acts as one who is distressed or afflicted.

Thus the wise man is willing to accept every appropriate kind of behaviour as his own.

When in a high position, he does not regard his inferiors with contempt. When in a low position, he does not flatter his superiors.

He always acts appropriately of his own accord, and needs no guidance by others. Hence, he does not feel himself imposed upon. He neither grumbles about his cosmic fate nor complains about his treatment by men.

Thus the wise man is serene and confident, trusting the future. But the foolish man risks troubles, hoping for more than he deserves. The wise man is like an archer. When the archer fails to hit the target, he reflects and looks for the cause of his failure within himself.

START AT THE SOURCE

The nature of a wise man is something like going on a long journey, since in order to go far he must first go through what is near, and is something like climbing a high peak, since in order to attain the top he must first start at the bottom.

In the *Book of Verses* it is written: 'Happy association with wife and children is like the music of lutes and harps. When cordiality prevails among brothers, the harmony is pleasing and gratifying. With your household harmoniously organised, enjoy the companionship of your wife and children.'

In such circumstances, parents enjoy contentment.

WISDOM IS INVISIBLE

How profusely do invisible powers manifest their influence!

When we look for them, we cannot see them. Yet they are present everywhere, and nothing is without them.

They move masses of people to fast and to purify themselves and to bedeck themselves with their finest raiment in order to sacrifice to them. The world seems flooded with them, both above and on all sides.

In the *Book of Verses* it is written: 'The invisible powers come upon us unawares. Yet they cannot be ignored.'

Such is the way in which the invisible is expressed. And such is the impossibility of restraining expressions of faith.

WISDOM IS MOST WORTHY

Nature, in creating all things, provides for them according to their capacities. Thus it nourishes that which is flourishing, and brings to its end that which is declining.

In the *Book of Verses* it is written: 'The revered and gracious leader exemplifies illustrious character. He organises his people and co-ordinates his officers. He benefits from Nature's providence. Nature protects him, helps him, and elevates him. Nature supports him continuously.'

So it is that he who possesses a virtuous character will receive a high calling.

THE WISE ARE CONSIDERATE

Now filial considerateness consists in diligently fulfilling the desires of one's fathers and in perpetuating their achievements.

To occupy the same places which our fathers occupied, to perform the ceremonies just as they did, to play the same music which they played, to honour those whom they honoured, to love those

115

whom they loved; and to respect those who are dead as they were respected when alive and to regard the departed as still as worthy as if they were with us – this is the perfect exemplification of filial considerateness.

By performing the seasonal ceremonies, we pay our appropriate respects to the cosmic forces, and by performing memorial services, we pay our appropriate respects to our ancestral progenitors. He who comprehends the significance of the seasonal ceremonies and of the memorial ceremonies is as fit to govern a kingdom as to care for his own hand.

GOOD GOVERNMENT DEPENDS ON GOOD MEN

When good men are in office, government is efficient, just as when the earth is fertile, plants flourish.

Therefore, good government depends upon good men. Such men should be chosen on the basis of character. Good character is developed by following the way. By following too, one acquires good will.

Good will is essential to being human, and it emerges first in caring for one's family. The best way of doing things is to recognise each thing for what it is, especially for its true worth. Just as there are differences in the care with which we treat closer and more distant relatives, so we should recognise differences in merit for different levels of responsibility, and accept them in social practice.

When those who are governed do not have confidence in their governors, they cannot be controlled.

Therefore a leader ought not to neglect the development of his own character. In endeavouring to develop his character, he should not fail to acquire an understanding of human nature. By achieving and understanding of the nature of man, he does not fail to gain insight into Nature.

The nature of social (i.e. mutual) relationships may be illustrated by five social relationships, and the characteristics needed to fulfil them may be summarised as three.

The relationships are those 1) between sovereign and subject, 2) between father and son, 3) between husband and wife, 4) between elder brother and younger brother, and 5) between friend and friend associating as equals. These five exemplify the nature of all social relationships.

The three traits – concern (*chih*), good will (*jen*), and conscientiousness (*yung*) – are required in all social relationships. In effect, the way in which these three traits function is unitary.

Some persons seem born with social aptitudes. Some acquire them by learning from teachers. And some develop them through trial-and-error experiences. But no matter how obtained, they operate in the same way.

Some persons express their concern for others spontaneously, some by calculating the rewards in prospect, and some by reluctantly forcing themselves. But when concern and good will and conscientiousness for others are expressed, then, regardless of whether they are expressed spontaneously, calculatingly, or reluctantly, the results are the same.

To be fond of learning is close to having wisdom (*chih*). To try hard is close to having good will (*jen*). To have feelings of guilt contributes to conscientiousness (*yung*).

When a person understands these traits, then he knows how to develop his character. When he knows how to develop his character, then he knows how to guide others. When he knows how to guide others, then he knows how to govern the whole country, including its states and communities.

Whoever is responsible for governing the whole country, including its states and communities, has nine principles to practise:

1) the development of his own character
2) recognition of those who are worthy
3) expressing due affection for his relatives
4) having complete confidence in his most responsible officials
5) taking a personal interest in the problems of all other public officials
6) paternal treatment of the common people
7) the fostering of manufacturers and tradesmen
8) gracious entertainment of foreigners
9) appreciating the services of political leaders

When a governor develops his own character, he thereby secures the operation of Nature's way (*tao*) in his realm.

When he recognises those who are worthy, he avoids the evil of favouritism.

When he expresses due affection for his relatives, they will have no reason for complaint.

When he has complete confidence in his most responsible officials, he will refrain from meddling in their affairs.

When he takes a personal interest in the problems of all other public officials, he earns their personal gratitude.

When he treats the common people with a paternal attitude, then their morale improves.

When he fosters manufacturing and trade, the country will prosper.

When he entertains foreigners graciously, people from everywhere will be attracted to him.

And when he appreciates the services of political leaders, then the whole country remains loyal to him.

By self-restraint, cleanliness, neatness in dress, and refraining from all inappropriate behaviour – this is the way for a leader to develop his character.

By ignoring slander, remaining unresponsive to enticements, disregarding riches, and acknowledging accomplishments – this is the way to recognise those who are worthy.

By respecting their positions, helping them to become well off, and sympathising with their preferences – this is the way to express due affection for one's relatives.

By giving them a free hand and full authority to carry out their duties – this is the way to have complete confidence in the most reliable officials.

By assuring them of job security and providing them with good salaries – this is the way to take a personal interest in the problems of all other public officials.

By requiring public celebrations only on regular holidays and lowering their taxes – this is the way to improve the morale of the common people.

By daily supervision and monthly inspections to ensure fair wages and just prices – this is the way to foster manufacturers and tradesmen.

By greeting them upon arrival and escorting them when they depart, and by praising their proficiency and forgiving their inexperience – this is the way to entertain foreigners graciously.

By restoring to honour the families of former governors, by reinstating control in states where the government has collapsed, by re-establishing order in states which have become chaotic and by protecting those who are in danger, by conducting councils of representatives of the states at regular intervals, by requiring them to bring in only small assessments and sending them away with large appropriations – this is the way to appreciate the services of political leaders.

These, then, are the nine principles for successful practice for all who have to govern a country or a state or a community. Success results from using all of them in the spirit of genuineness.

In all affairs, achievement depends upon previous preparation; without such preparation, failure is certain. When one decides beforehand what one wants to say, then one's speech will not falter. When one determines beforehand how one wishes to deal with things, one will not meet trouble later. When one plans one's course of action, one will not become perplexed. When one employs the best ways of proceeding (*tao*) habitually, then one will profit from them perpetually.

When those who are governed do not have confidence in their governors, they cannot be controlled.

But there is a way for a governor to gain such confidence:

First he should recognise the principle that if he cannot be trusted by his friends, then he will not be trusted by those whom he governs.

There is a way to gain the confidence of one's friends: One should recognise the principle that if one is not faithful to one's parents, then one will not be trusted by one's friends.

There is a way to be faithful to one's parents: One should recognise the principle that if one is not honest with oneself, then one cannot be faithful to one's parents.

There is a way to be honest with oneself: One should recognise the principle that if one does not know what is good, then one cannot be honest with oneself.

Nature's way is to *be* genuine. Man's way is to *become* genuine.

To be genuine is to act truly without effort, to attain without thinking about it, and automatically and spontaneously to realise one's genuine nature. Such a man is wise.

To become genuine is to try to do what is good and to keep on trying.

In order to do this, one must first thoroughly investigate the nature of what is good, earnestly inquiring about it, meticulously examining it, clearly formulating a conception of it, and diligently learning from practical experience with it.

So long as there is anything which one has not investigated, one will not cease in one's efforts.

So long as there is anything which one has not thoroughly examined, or anything in what one has examined which one does not understand, one will not cease in one's efforts.

So long as there is anything of which one has not formulated a clear conception, or anything in such a conception which one does not understand, one will not cease in one's efforts.

So long as there is anything which one has not tried out in practical experience, or anything in such experience which one does not understand, one will not cease in his efforts.

Even though others may succeed with a single effort, one will put forth a hundred efforts if necessary, and where others succeed with ten attempts, one will make a thousand attempts if necessary.

Whoever follows this way, even though he be sluggish, he will achieve understanding; even though he is weak, he will attain strength.

TWO SOURCES OF GENUINENESS

When our understanding springs from our genuineness, it may be said to emerge from our nature.

When our genuineness is derived from our understanding, it may be said to result from education.

From genuineness we may develop understanding and from understanding we may acquire genuineness.

HOW TO INFLUENCE THE WORLD

It is only he who is completely genuine in the affairs of this world who can develop his own nature to its fullest.

If he can develop his own nature to its fullest, then he can help in the full development of the natures of other men.

If he can help in the full development of other men's natures, then he can help in the full development of the natures of all animate and inanimate beings.

If he can help in the full development of all animate and inanimate beings, then he can help in the production and maturation activities of Nature above and Nature below.

When he helps in the production and maturation of Nature above and Nature below, he likewise becomes a creative agent in the universe.

HOPE FOR THE PARTLY GENUINE

Next is he who develops genuineness only partially. From this, he can experience the nature of genuineness.

In this way, the nature of genuineness becomes actualised in him.

When it becomes actualised in him, then it becomes apparent to him.

When it becomes apparent to him, then it becomes clear to others also.

When it becomes clear to others also, then it influences them.

When it influences others, they are moulded by it.

When they are moulded by it, they are improved.

It is only he who is completely genuine in the affairs of this world who can improve others.

ACHIEVING PREDICTIVE POWER

It is a natural consequence for a completely genuine man to be able to predict the course of things.

When a nation or a family is about to become prosperous, evidences of good tendencies are certain to appear, and when it is about to become ruined, evidences of evil tendencies appear.

It can be seen both in external means of prognostication and in how they affect one's bodily behaviour.

When ruin or prosperity is in prospect, he can surely foresee both good and evil outcomes. Therefore, the completely genuine man is like one having superior powers.

GENUINENESS IMPROVES BOTH SELF AND OTHERS

Genuineness is self-sufficient. And its nature is self-directing.

Genuineness pervades being from beginning to end. Without genuineness, nothing could be done. This is why the wise man values becoming genuine above everything else.

The person who tries to be genuine not only promotes his own self-realisation. He also promotes the self-realisation of others.

Self-realisation involves associating with others (*jen*). Developing one's relations with others involves sympathy. Both associating with others and having sympathy are abilities which anything has for realising its own nature (*teh*).

One's whole nature (*tao*) integrates both external relations and inner processes. Hence, genuineness is fully genuine when both of these abilities are appropriately integrated.

GENUINENESS IS ALL-PERVADING

Therefore, what is most genuine pervades everything without ceasing.

Being unceasing, it is everlasting. Being everlasting, it is self-sufficient.

Being self-sufficient, it is all-inclusive. Being all-inclusive, it extends everywhere and is self-sustaining. Extending everywhere and being self-sustaining, it ascends high and shines forth.

By extending everywhere and being self-sustaining, it contains everything. By ascending high and shining forth, it covers everything. Being all-inclusive and everlasting, it brings all things to their completion.

By extending everywhere and being self-sustaining, it appears as the whole earth. By ascending high and shining forth, it appears in the heavens. By being all-inclusive, it is without limit.

Such is the nature of genuineness. Even though it is invisible, it produces all changes. Even though it exerts no effort, it accomplishes everything.

The nature (*tao*) of Nature may be summed up in one word: 'genuineness'. It is free from duplicity. How it does what it does is a mystery.

The nature of Nature is such that it extends everywhere and is self-sustaining, ascends high and shines forth, and is all-inclusive and everlasting.

That bit of heaven which appears above us now is only the visible portion of the sky. But when thought of as unlimited, encompassing the sun and moon, stars and galaxies, it overarches every-thing.

This bit of earth here under us is but a handful of dirt. Yet when considered in its breadth and depth, it supports heavy mountains without strain and retains rivers and oceans without letting them drain away.

This mountain here before us looks like a mere pile of rocks; yet on its broad slopes grow grass and trees, birds and animals make their homes on it, and stores of valuable minerals abound within it.

This lake here before us seems like a mere dipperful; yet in its bottomless depths swim myriads of fishes and turtles and sharks. Bountiful resources swarm within it.

In the *Book of Verses* it is written: 'The provisions of Heaven! How plenteous and unfailing!' This means that such plenitude and end-less supply is what makes Heaven Heaven, or the nature of Nature.

SUPERIORITY OF THE SAGE

How superior the nature of sageliness!

Bountiful as the ocean, it can stimulate and inspire all living beings,and ascend to the heights of Heaven.

How proficient is its superiority!

It masters all of the principles of propriety and all of the rules of etiquette.

It awaits the right man, and then it becomes actualised.

Hence it is said: 'Unless one has the ability to follow nature (*teh*) completely, nature (*tao*) cannot function perfectly.'

Therefore, the wise man prizes his ability to follow nature with-out deviation (*teh*). He persists in self-examination and inquiry into the needs of others, trying to pursue it to its fullest breadth, yet giving attention to its finest details, and striving to develop it to its highest excellence. In this way he develops his genuine self (*chung yung*). This is the reason why he both studies ancient history and is alert to the latest news. He is genuinely interested in both respect for and practice of whatever is right (*li*).

So, while holding a high position, he is not haughty, and when he finds himself in a low position, he does not complain.

When social conditions are naturally wholesome (*tao*), his advice is admired. When social conditions become disorderly, he is tolerated if he maintains his silence.

Is not this the significance of the *Book of Verses* when it says: 'By wisdom and discretion he perpetuates himself'?

ABILITY NEEDED FOR RESPONSIBILITY

One who is uninformed and yet opinionated, one who is incapable of caring for himself and yet wants to have his own way, and one who faces present problems and yet refuses to profit by past experiences – all such people are courting disaster.

If one occupies a position of responsibility but lacks the necessary capacity, one ought not to revise the established procedures or standards of taste. If one has the capacity but lacks the position of authority, one cannot revise the system of procedure or artistic standards.

HOW A SAGE GENERATES CONFIDENCE

No matter how excellent the ancient customs, if they cannot be tried out today, their value cannot be demonstrated. Without demonstration, people will not follow them.

No matter how excellent the moral advice coming from those who lack prestige, it will not be respected. Without such respect, people will not have faith in them. Without such faith, people will not follow them.

Therefore, the regulations promulgated by a sage leader should be founded upon his own character and experience, and they should be adequately demonstrated in the lives of the people. They should be verified historically to see whether they are deficient. They should be displayed before departed ancestors without fear or hesitation. They should be felt worthy of scrutiny by sages centuries later, without any uncertainty.

By displaying his regulations before departed ancestors without fear or hesitation, the wise leader demonstrates his knowledge of Heaven. By being willing, without feeling uncertain, to await the scrutiny of sages centuries later, he demonstrates his knowledge of men.

When this is so, then the deportment of the leader serves as a model, his conduct is regarded as a standard, and his language serves as an example before the whole country for generations. Those who are distant from him admire him, and those close to him never tire of him.

In the *Book of Verses* it is written: 'Without animosity there, without boredom here, day after day, night after night, they recite his praises.'

No wise man, without earning such laudation, ever became famous throughout the ancient world.

MAGNIFICENCE OF NATURE'S WAY

Nature harmonizes with the reliable rhythms of heaven above, and is consistent with the regularities in the earth and water below.

In their inclusiveness and sustainingness, and in their comprehensiveness and protectiveness, they are comparable to Heaven and Earth.

In the orderliness of procedures, they are comparable to day and night and the four seasons. Nature shows how all things flourish together without harming each other. Each thing follows its own nature (*tao*) without interfering with others. Lesser things such as rivulets follow their own courses, while at the same time greater processes such as day and night and the four seasons pursue their tremendous transformations. This is why Nature is so magnificent.

THE SAGE HAS DEPTH AND BREADTH

Only the most sage person in the world can unite in himself the quickness, clarity, breadth, and depth of understanding needed for guiding men; the magnanimity, generosity, benevolence, and gentleness needed for getting along with others; the attentiveness, strength, stability, and tenacity needed for maintaining control; the serenity, seriousness, unwaveringness, and propriety needed for commanding respect; and the well-informedness, methodicalness, thoroughness, and penetration needed for exercising sound judgment.

Because he exercises his abilities when they are needed, he is able to do all kinds of things, to serve wide areas, to penetrate deeply, and to flow on perpetually.

In being able to do all kinds of things and to serve wide areas, he is like Heaven. In penetrating deeply and flowing on perpetually, he is like the ocean. Whenever he appears, everyone adores him. Whatever he says, everyone trusts him. Whatever he does, everyone is grateful to him.

Consequently, his fame spreads throughout the country and extends to foreign lands. Wherever carts and boats go, wherever human enterprise penetrates, wherever the sky reaches and the earth extends, wherever the sun and moon shine, and wherever the frost and dew settle – all who live and breathe honour him.

THE SAGE IS WHOLE-HEARTED

Only the most completely genuine man in the world is able to harmonise the opposing strands of human society, to establish and maintain moral order in the country, and to understand the developing and maturing processes of Nature. Need such a person depend upon anything outside himself?

How whole-hearted his good will!
Who can comprehend such a man unless he himself has quickness, clarity, breadth and depth of understanding, and breadth of perspective?

THE SAGE IS HUMBLE

In the *Book of Verses* it is written: 'Over her ornate gown she wears an ordinary dress', implying dislike for ostentation. Similarly, it is the nature of a wise man to refrain from ostentation, while gaining in renown daily; whereas it is the nature of the foolish man to seek notoriety, while gaining disrepute daily.

The wise man does not appear exciting, yet people never become bored with him. Although seeming simple, he is really intricate. Although apparently friendly, he remains serious. He knows that attainment of distant goals comes through attentiveness to things near at hand. He knows the causes of things. He knows how little things grow into big things. Such a person embodies a sound character.

In the *Book of Verses* it is written: 'That which is deep and foundational may still be quite apparent.' Therefore the wise man scrutinises his inmost self, to eradicate evil and to eliminate inadequacy. That in which the wise man is unexcelled cannot fail to be seen by other men.

In the *Book of Verses* it is written: 'Even when secluded in privacy, be free from guilt, for you are visible in light from above.' Therefore, the wise man continues to have high regard for good behaviour even when he is inactive, and for truthfulness even when he is silent.

In the *Book of Verses* it is written: 'One worships without asking for reward.' Therefore, the wise man does not offer enticements, and still the people are uplifted. He does not express anger, and yet they are moved more than if threatened with hatchets and clubs.

In the *Book of Verses* it is written: 'Good character does not need to be advertised. Noble men seek it anyway.' Therefore, when the wise man remains genuine and attentive, the whole world attains peace.

In the *Book of Verses* it is written: 'I admire your excellent character. How unpretentious – neither loud nor showy.' Among the means of influencing people, loudness and showiness are least effective.

Again in the *Book of Verses* it is written: 'Character is as unobtrusive as a hair.' Yet even a hair can be obtrusive in some degree. 'The actions of Heaven are without sound or odour.' That is perfection.

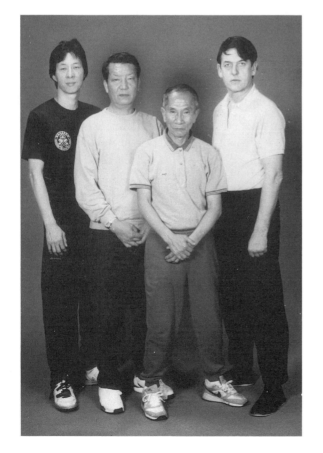

Yip Chun spends time in Hong Kong and in England. Anyone wishing to study Wing Chun with Grandmaster Yip Chun should address correspondence to the Wing Chun Athletic Association, 18 Swan Street, Manchester, M4 5JN, England. The chief instructor is Mr. Samuel Kwok, pictured here with fellow teacher Yip Ching, along with Yip Chun and Danny Connor.

APPENDIX:
WING CHUN
TERMINOLOGY

Siu Lim Tao (1st form) — little idea
Chum Kiu (2nd form) — arm seeking
Biu Tze (3rd form) — thrusting fingers
Muk Yan Chong — wooden man
Chi Dan Sau — single-hand sticking
Chi Sau — arm clinging exercise

bong sau — wing arm
gum sau — pinning hand
fak sau — whisking arm
fook sau — bridge on arm
gaun sau — low block
huen sau — circling hand
jum sau — sinking block
jut sau — jerk hand
kau sau — circling block
kwun sau — rotating arms
lan sau — bar arm
lap sau — pulling arm
lin wan kuen — chain punches

mun sau — inquisitive arm
pak sau — slap block
pie jarn — elbow hacking
po pai — double arms
tan sau — palm up arm
wu sau — protective arm
biu sau — thrusting hand
chair pie — diagonal elbow strike
gung lik — forward elbow energy
gwoy jarn — horizontal elbow strike
gor sau — free hand technique
jic seen — centre line
jing jeung — vertical palm strike
kup jarn — downward elbow strike
si-fu — teacher, father
sung lik — relax
tok sau — lifting hand technique
wang jeung — side palm strike
yat chi kuen — single front punch
yee gee kim yeung ma — basic stance position